Within the covers of this book is all the advice you will need to start you sailing.

How to choose a boat; how to maintain it; how to sail it.

Crystal-clear instructions and skilfully designed illustrations will have you sailing in less time than you thought possible.

After an eventful career in the Royal Navy the author, Commander Hewitt, became Superintendent of the Navy League's Training Centre, where he coached thousands of novices in the handling of small boats.

Sailing a Small Boat

Commander
F. J. G. Hewitt, D.S.C.

FUTURA PUBLICATIONS
A Pocket Guide

Futura Publications Limited
110 Warner Road
Camberwell, London SE5

A Pocket Guide

First published in this revised
edition in Great Britain in 1977

First published in original edition
in Great Britain in 1962 by Oldbourne

ISBN 0 7088 0977 4

Printed in Great Britain by
Hazell Watson & Viney Ltd
Aylesbury, Bucks

Contents

Introduction

When a man takes up motoring he realises that he must take lessons in driving. Besides learning how to manipulate the gears he has to acquire some road sense. In due course he has to satisfy an examiner that he knows what he is doing.

At the present time you do not have to pass a test and satisfy authorities that you are capable of handling a boat, but you will be wise to study the elementary principles and prepare yourself for what is involved, before you take charge of a sailing boat.

There are many thousands of people who wish to take up sailing and want to know how to set about it. It is not much use telling them that one of the best ways is to serve as crew to an expert helmsman for a season or two. For one thing the opportunity may not arise, and, in any case, this method takes time. Understandably they are impatient to make a start. One sympathises with their eagerness and appreciates the bewilderment that holds them back.

They see so many varieties of sailing boat, small and large, racing and cruising boats. Whatever may be the beginner's ultimate objective it is clear that he should explore the principles of sailing as a beginning. This book will help him over the first steps.

As far as possible I shall steer clear of complicated nautical terms and jargon in the early stages and set our course towards an understanding of basic principles. Some technical terms cannot be avoided or we shall get into a muddle.

To begin with I am going to make the assumption that you can swim. Never let it be said that this book encouraged anyone to take up boating unless he could look after himself in the water. The non-swimmer in a boat is a nuisance not only to himself but to others in the vicinity. Nobody expects the boating enthusiast to be a channel swimmer, but he should have enough confidence in the water to avoid panic.

Right, let's get started . . .

Chapter One
Getting Acquainted

One of your constant problems will be to keep to a good mean course. There are many different types of boat. There are also endless variations in fittings and rigs and in styles and techniques. My concern will be to look after the basic principles and let the variations look after themselves.

Before you get involved in the use of sails you must understand the behaviour of a boat in the water: how it floats and what happens to it under different conditions. You can study this quite well in a small rowing boat.

It is a simple technique and does not warrant much space in this book. Largely it is a matter of practice which can be put in on the local lake or boating pond. You may, if you wish, take someone with you and let him sit in the stern and steer the boat with the rudder, but except for encouragement this isn't really necessary. In fact you must learn to steer your boat while you are manipulating the oars.

It may be that you feel quite a stranger to boats of any kind. In which case you had better learn first to pull a single

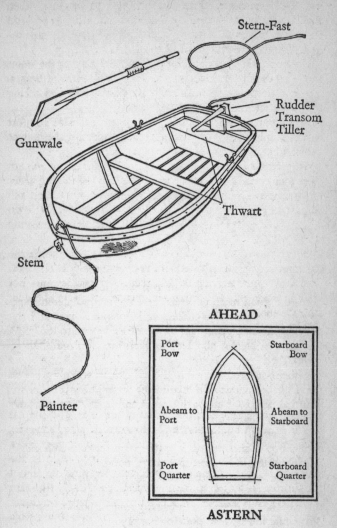

Stern-Fast

Rudder
Transom
Tiller

Gunwale

Thwart

Stem

Painter

AHEAD

Port Bow		Starboard Bow
Abeam to Port		Abeam to Starboard
Port Quarter		Starboard Quarter

ASTERN

Fig 1. Rowing Boat

oar. This means you must enrol someone to go along when you hire the boat. You will pull on one side while he pulls on the other. You will learn to keep stroke (to pull in time together) and the best methods of stopping and turning.

To stop (take the way off) you dip the blades in the water and hold them there like brakes. They make efficient brakes. You can do more: you can drive the boat astern by backing the oars through the water.

While you are at the boating lake you can derive comfort as you watch so many of our island race disporting themselves and making mistakes which you will avoid.

To turn the boat and change its direction it is not enough to pull on one side only. You assist the turn by holding water or backing on one side while you pull on the other. You will see that it is quite easy to turn the boat around in its own length by this method. These things must become second nature to you.

In my part of the world it is the fashion to row while the oarsman sits on the thwarts with his back towards the bows. This is all right so long as you remember that you are not looking where you are going and glance over your shoulder from time to time.

As you get the idea, you can progress to the stage of handling the boat with two oars by yourself. Then you will be nearly ready for other things.

You are now on the way to understanding an interesting characteristic of the turning properties of a boat. It differs markedly from a bicycle or motor car. When you spin the steering wheel of a car, the front wheels turn and the car follows round more or less in their tracks. A boat, however, turns on a pivot. When it is stopped the boat pivots round a point midway along its length. When it has way on it, the boat pivots on a point which is further forward, say about one third of its length from the stem. Consequently the stern of the boat does most of the movement and swings outwards rather like a skid. The longer the boat, the more noticeable this becomes.

Every boat deserves careful handling. You should aim to

bring it alongside the bank, or a jetty or another boat, smoothly and gently, not with a series of bumps. On your boating lake you will see many people making a mess of it. For one thing they are sometimes puzzled because the oars seem to be in the way. You may see them come into the bank at right angles, and, after hitting it with a thump, fumble about getting the oars unshipped and bringing the boat alongside.

One good method is to approach at a nice angle and speed so that you can get in the inside oar in good time; then hold water with the outer oar so as to bring up parallel to your berth and just clear of it. You should not let the side smack or scrape against the bank. In larger boats you will have fenders to prevent damage to the sides.

When you feel competent to handle a small rowing-boat on your own at the boating lake, you are ready to consider some of the other facts of sailing life. Among the most important are the effects of a stream or current. To explain this I'll transport you to a non-tidal river. Here you have to consider a fairly constant movement of water from the river's source down towards its mouth.

Sitting in the water without any way on it, your boat will go with the stream down river like any piece of flotsam. If it should meet up with a stationary object, like a buoy or a bridge or a vessel at anchor, it is liable to hit it as the stream takes it along.

If you propel the boat with the oars, your speed past stationary objects depends on the direction in which you are pulling. If you are going with the stream you will be travelling fast. If you are pulling against the stream it will be harder work and you will be travelling much more slowly 'over the ground'. But you will be safer and the boat will be more manoeuvrable.

Let me harp on this a bit, because while the principle is obvious to most people, it is frequently ignored or overlooked by others, and neglect of it can be dangerous.

Suppose the stream is running at two knots (two nautical miles per hour). If you pull your boat at a speed of three knots in the same direction as the stream you will be travelling at five knots. You will shoot through the arch of a bridge at five knots if your steering is good enough. If it is not, you may hit a pillar, damage the boat and finish up in the water.

If you turn around and pull against the stream at three knots you will make a speed of only one knot 'over the ground'. It will take you a lot longer to get anywhere but you will have a less hair-raising trip through the arch of that bridge.

The object of this homily has been to impress upon you that it is safer to head against the stream than to go with it. When you wish to take your boat away from the bank or to bring it back alongside it is always best to have the craft's head pointing up stream.

Consider what happens if you do it the wrong way. Heading down stream as you approach your berth you will find the stream carrying you along no matter what you do with the oars to take the way off. And you fetch up alongside with one of those nasty, jarring crunches that foretell damage and expense. The right way, heading into the stream, is much easier because the stream actually helps you to bring up nicely in your berth.

Later on I shall discuss other effects of stream, current and tides, but if you have stayed with me so far, you deserve to move on to another lesson.

Chapter Two
Consider the Theory

It is a mystery to some people how or why a boat sails at all, and to judge by incidents I see from time to time, this mystery persists not only among novices.

To give a little background to the subject let me briefly consider one or two high-lights in the development of sails.

From paintings and history books the reader will be familiar with the appearance of ancient galleons. These carried huge full-bellied sails which looked impressive but were not very efficient. The vessels could be driven along before good following winds but they were wholly dependent on favourable winds. The galleons of the Armada were blown up the English Channel into the North Sea long after they had changed their minds about the invasion; an early instance of foreign visitors being discomfited by English weather.

As time went by it was realised that large bellying sails were less efficient than smaller and flatter sails and that the latter were easier to handle. Not long ago famous barques and full-rigged ships, with towering spreads of canvas, made remarkable passages around the world. Most of their sails were hoisted on yards slung athwartships on the masts, so they were said to be 'square-rigged'. But they also had a number of 'fore-and-aft' sails, jibs, stay-sails and a spanker. Do not worry about these terms, they will become clear later.

The yards could be braced well round and, with the aid of the fore-and-aft sails, these vessels could be sailed very effectively with the wind abeam (coming from the side) and even with the wind two points (about twenty degrees) before the beam (coming from ahead). Their courses were therefore less restricted by wind direction.

With very few exceptions all modern sailing boats are fitted with 'fore-and-aft' rig only. As you watch them sail you will observe that they have great freedom to manoeuvre. You will see that they can make their way up or down river or in and out of harbour without being unduly perturbed by the direction of the wind. How is it done?

Let me attempt a simple explanation which can be demonstrated with a model yacht or a toy boat. In the interests of simplicity this explanation will not be absolutely accurate to begin with. Neither was the gooseberry bush theory given to you when you were very young, but it will serve just as well until you are ready for more advanced thinking.

Your model yacht may have one or two or more sails but, for the moment, I will consider only one, the large mainsail. The wind is blowing across the side from a direction at right angles to the keel: we say the wind is abeam.

If the sail is left loose and flapping the model will not move ahead at all. Now haul in the mainsheet until the sail is as taut as a board in the fore-and-aft line. The wind will try to blow the model sideways.

The model yacht resents this. It is not shaped to go sideways. There is, for instance, a keel which holds it in the water, a heavy metal or wooden shaft which protrudes from the bottom of the boat into the water. So the pressure of wind on the sail tends to push the yacht over. With enough wind the model will capsize.

This is all straightforward so far. Now comes the nub of the argument. Slack off the sheet so that the sail is at an angle of about forty-five degrees (half a right angle) from the fore-and-aft line. Now see what happens.

The wind's force will be resolved into two components. One still trying to blow the model sideways; the other, more successful, driving the boat ahead.

It may be that you do not like the tang of mathematics or the idea of resolving a force into two components. But it is important that you should grasp the principle as it will crop up in one form or another continuously. It would help, perhaps, if I give you a demonstration to clarify the action.

Take a piece of wet soap and place it on a flat surface. Press on the sloping edge of the soap with the side of the hand and notice how the soap shoots away at right angles to the pressure.

Of course, this will also explain why the soap eludes you in the bath. So I am not wasting time. But I hope it will reinforce the understanding in your mind of the result of the wind blowing on to the slanting surface of the sail.

So far I have been considering one sail only. Your model, and most of the sailing boats you will encounter, probably has two sails, a foresail and a mainsail. What we have discovered so far applies equally to each. There is also a certain amount of interplay between them, but I will leave this until later.

For the moment I want you to concentrate on the two fundamental rules which have emerged. You let go the sheets (ropes) and allow the sails to shake and flap if you do not want the boat to move. You haul them in when you want to sail ahead. The amount you haul them in depends on the direction of the wind. When it is coming from abeam the angle of the sail from the fore-and-aft line is roughly forty-five degrees.

When the boat is sailing with the wind abeam or nearly so, she is said to be 'reaching' or 'sailing on a reach'. Sometimes this may be qualified. For example, people talk of a 'broad reach' when the wind comes from a point or two further aft than the beam, but, as a beginner, you need not bother about these fine distinctions.

When the wind comes from over the boat's quarter or from

further aft, she is said to be 'running' or 'running with the wind aft'. Under these conditions there is a slight difference in technique which we must now consider.

It is much easier to understand how the boat sails in these circumstances, especially when the wind is right aft, i.e., coming over the stern of the boat, from behind. The effect of the wind pushing the boat along is the same as when paper bags are blown along a beach.

You ease out the sheets as the wind draws aft. With the wind right aft the sail obviously should be out on the beam

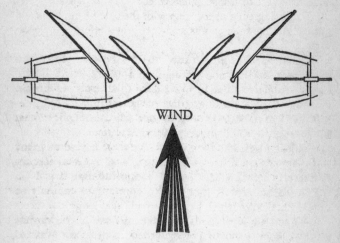

WIND

Fig 2. Reaching

at right angles to the fore-and-aft line (or the keel) in order to get the most efficiency from your sail area.

From which we arrive at a simple rule of thumb. The angle between the sail and the fore-and-aft line from aft is about half the angle between the direction of the wind and the fore-and-aft line from forward. Let me explain.

When you were reaching the wind was coming over the beam, that is to say, the angle from forward was ninety degrees, a right angle. I told you that the sail should be about

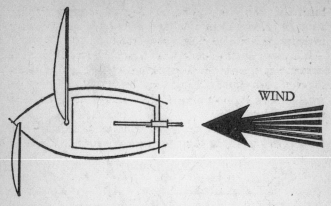

WIND

Fig 3. Running with wind aft

forty-five degrees, half a right angle, from the fore-and-aft line.

With the wind aft the angle is one hundred and eighty degrees, two right angles from forward. So the sail angle from aft should be ninety degrees or one right angle.

Ponder on this for a minute, because there is method in my seeming madness. I am not suggesting that you should equip yourself with a protractor when you go sailing. And I am aware that the sail sets in a curve so that angles can only be judged very roughly.

The object of giving you this rule of thumb is to impress on your mind that your sails must be continually adjusted according to the direction of the wind. So many beginners forget this. Too often I see them altering course and sailing before the wind with the sails still hauled in taut. As I shall explain later, this may cause trouble. *So!* Keep the rule of thumb in your mind and remember to adjust your sheets.

Now you are ready to study the art of beating to windward.

It is a fair guess that sailing would be less interesting if we could sail only with the wind aft or on the beam. Fortunately boats can be sailed up to windward, against the wind. A boat with a fore-and-aft rig can be sailed as close as forty-five degrees, half a right angle, to the wind quite comfortably. But

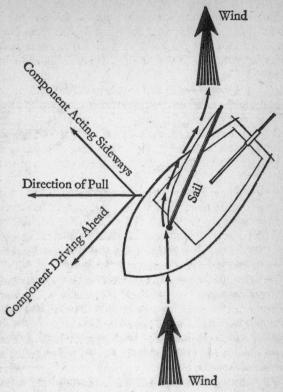

Fig 4. Beating to Windward

no closer, although you would be surprised at the number of people who try.

To get a boat up to windward the drill is to sail in a series of diagonals first on one side of the wind then the other, until you reach journey's end. The process is known as tacking or beating to windward. The boat is said to be on the port tack when the wind is coming over the port bow. And, of course, on the starboard tack when the wind comes over the starboard bow.

Our rule of thumb about the angle of the sail still holds good. The wind direction is forty-five degrees from forward; therefore the sail angle should be half of this, twenty-odd degrees from aft. This means, in effect, that the sheets are hauled in tight.

How the boat sails in this way is more difficult to understand, and the time has come to enlarge upon my explanation of the effect of the wind pushing on the sails.

As you have noticed, the sails are not flat like boards but are set in graceful curves. It is these curves which perform the magic. They have something of the properties of an aeroplane's wing.

An aeroplane flies because of the airflow over the top of its wing and not because of a push on the under side. There is a similar influence when the wind skids past the outside of the curve of a sail. Not entirely, because the sail has not got all the shape of an aeroplane wing; but it is enough for you to consider that the wind exerts a pull on the sail.

Let us not become too immersed in scientific principles. Suffice to say that you may find it easier to understand the performance of your boat up to windward if you think in terms of a pull on the sails rather than a push.

If, on the other hand, you find this too difficult, do not lose any sleep over it. There is no harm in still considering as we have all along, that the wind is giving a push. What you must not forget is that the force is still to be regarded as having two components. One driving the boat ahead and the other trying to push it sideways.

In this case the sideways component is important. You have to counteract it effectively or the boat will not sail at all. In a small boat the keel is not enough, so there is an extra gadget called a centre-plate which is lowered through a slot in the bottom of the boat (and enclosed in a box). This gives more lateral resistance in the water.

I shall discuss centre-plates more fully in a later chapter, but I think you have had enough theory for the time being. It is important that you should get back to practical problems, so let us find ourselves a boat.

Chapter Three
Getting the Boat Ready

Choosing a boat is in itself a problem. For many beginners it is decided by what is available at the local club or boat pool. Others may wish to buy a boat straight away. Be cautious about this. There are cruising boats, day boats, racing types, large, small, old and new boats to be had, but you can hardly form a lasting opinion of what will suit you best until you know a bit more about sailing. It is better, if you can, to leave your money in the old oak chest until you have had the chance to try out different types of boat.

If you have the opportunity of choosing, you will do well in my opinion to select a sturdy and stable boat for your early training rather than the light racing type. Such a boat will give you more time to think and act in the various circumstances that will arise. This is better than coming to the surface after a capsize and pondering on what you should have done.

For much the same reasons it is prudent to go on your first few trips when the wind is light and steady and when the stream, if any, is gentle. Then you will be able to learn your sailing step by step. Flurry and panic are not good teachers.

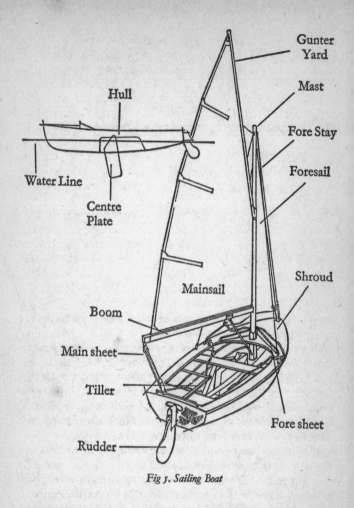

Gunter Yard

Mast

Hull

Fore Stay

Foresail

Water Line

Centre Plate

Shroud

Mainsail

Boom

Main sheet

Tiller

Fore sheet

Rudder

Fig 5. Sailing Boat

I will assume you have found a boat, about fourteen feet long and with a beam (breadth) of about six feet. You are going to get it ready for your first trip.

You will need a reliable companion as your crew. Here again the local yacht club may provide an answer. For your first trip you should try to find an experienced sailor. As you progress, you can afford to be less particular, but a first trip with two novices on board should be avoided.

Both of you can swim. Even so, equip yourselves with lifejackets. This is not pessimism. It is a sound rule that you should wear a lifejacket while you are sailing. There are obvious reasons. An accidental thump on the head might be one. The weight of your warm clothing another. But a further very good reason is that a lifejacket helps you to float higher out of the water; if you capsize this will give you more leverage so that you will be better able to right the boat and get it sailing again.

The boat is lying alongside a jetty. The mast is shipped and you will notice that it is supported by a forestay and two shrouds. (See Fig 5.) You ship the rudder by sliding it on to gudgeons and pintles on the transom. Don't let these terms disturb you; it is perfectly obvious how the rudder is fitted into place. You fit the tiller to the rudder. Next you lower the centre-plate. You do this to make sure it is free and to become acquainted with its working. You wouldn't want to find it was jammed after you got under way.

Lowering the centre-plate increases your draught, remember, but you have plenty of water here so leave it down.

You have already learned in pulling-boats that it is desirable to leave the jetty with the bows pointing up stream. In a sailing boat another factor must be considered. The sails, particularly the mainsail, should be hoisted while the boat's head is pointed into the wind. Indeed, in some boats you may find that it is practically impossible to get the mainsail up unless the boat is in this position or nearly so.

Clearly you will come across occasions when these requirements are in conflict. I shall discuss such complications later. At this particular moment you are lucky. The boat is pointing up stream and the light breeze is coming from that direction too. You are all set to hoist the sails.

The foresail (sometimes called the jib) slides up the forestay on hanks attached to its leading edge (called the luff). It is hoisted by the fore halyard, a rope which runs through a

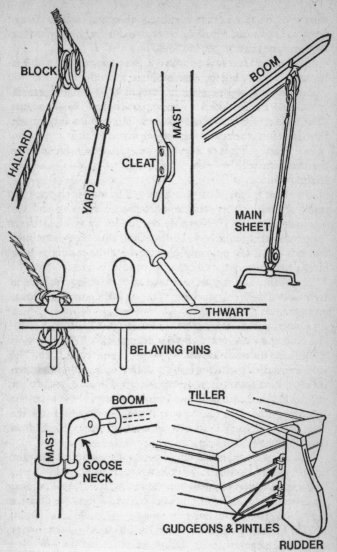

Fig 6. Fittings

sheave or block near the masthead, then comes back down again to be secured (made fast) on a cleat or belaying pin near its foot. (See Fig 6.)

It is well to see that the foresail is clear for hoisting but it is better to hoist it after the mainsail is set.

In this boat the mainsail is hauled up by two halyards secured to a spar called a gunter yard. These halyards also pass through sheaves or blocks at the masthead and are made fast on cleats or belaying pins near its foot.

Once again I must point out that different boats have different arrangements and, indeed, different types of sails, but the general idea is the same. What is most important at this stage is that you should know and be able to identify quickly each halyard in your boat and recognize its particular job. In emergency you may have to let go any one of them or all of them quickly. But in the ordinary run of things you may find that you don't have to touch them again until you come back alongside.

This is because the normal way of controlling the sails is by the sheets. In case you didn't know, the sheets are ropes, and not the sails themselves. To understand them you must first take a quick look at the sails now they are hoisted.

The leading edge of the foresail (called the luff) is held in position by the forestay. (See Fig 5.) It is a triangular sail. The lower corner of the luff (called the tack) is secured to the stem of the boat. The other corner of the foot of the sail is the clew and to this are attached two lengths of rope; these are the foresail sheets. One length is laid out on either side of the mast because, as you will see, the sail will be controlled on one side or the other of the boat when you are sailing.

The mainsail in this boat is rectangular although the yard is hoisted right up to make it nearly triangular. (See Fig 5.) The leading edge (again called the luff) which is not secured to the yard is usually kept in position close to the mast by a light lashing or by hoops or some other arrangement. Again, the lower corner of the luff is called the tack and the other corner at the foot of the sail is called the clew.

Before I pass on, you should note that the luffs of both

sails are always stretched taut because they are important to the performance of the sails when the boat is going to windward. I discussed earlier the analogy of the aeroplane's wing so you will understand why the leading edges of the sails play such an important part.

In your boat the foot of the mainsail is stretched along a boom and this is the usual practice nowadays. When a boom isn't fitted the mainsail is said to be 'loose-footed'.

The mainsheet is attached to the boom near the clew of the mainsail. It often takes the form of a tackle, that is to say, the rope passes through one, two or more blocks and these help when hauling in. The weight of the mainsail can be quite considerable when the wind is in it and it would be fatiguing to control the sail with a single rope. The tackle gives a mechanical advantage and eases the strain.

But it needs watching or it may get you into trouble. It should always be free and clear to run out. The tackle should not be so powerful that the sail cannot pull it out readily when you let go during the heavy pressure of a squall. You can test this without waiting for bad weather by pushing out on the boom.

This is as good a time as any to tell you and impress upon you that the mainsheet in a small boat is never made fast. It is always held in hand and should be free and clear to ease out or let go quickly.

There is one more feature appertaining to the sails which it is imperative that you understand before you are ready to go. This is the method of reefing.

It is hardly necessary to emphasise that in this country we never can be sure what the weather is going to do. If there is any suspicion that the wind is going to increase and blow too hard, you must reef the sails, which is to say you must reduce the effective sail area. On your first trip especially, it is better to have too little sail than too much.

There are various ways of reducing sail area but for the present I will treat the matter simply. In this boat your mainsail is fitted with a boom, so all you have to do is to roll the sail round the boom for two or three turns. There is a short length of rope near the tack which you use to prevent the turns unrolling.

The foresail hasn't got a boom, so the method is different. You will find one or two rows of 'reef points' (pieces of small rope) running parallel with the foot of the sail. In line with them are metal rings called cringles, on each edge of the sail. I shall tell you more about these fittings later but for the present you will see that the sail can be folded up from the foot and tied so that the effective area is reduced.

Now I shall keep you no longer from that exciting event, your first trip.

Chapter Four

First Trip
Beating to Windward

You are ready and the great moment has arrived. The rudder and tiller are in place, the centre plate is down and your sails are hoisted. They are flapping because the wind is coming from right ahead. Your boat is held alongside the jetty by two ropes, the painter (or head rope) and the stern-fast. You slip these and shove the bow well off.

You are the helmsman so you sit in the after part of the boat on the weather side, that is to say, the side over which the wind is coming or will be coming; you will be able to feel the wind on your back. The tiller is held with one hand, the mainsheet with the other. Your companion is further forward, controlling the foresail sheets and ready for odd jobs. He will sit in the middle line or out on the weather side to help in balancing the boat according to the strength of the wind.

As the bow is pushed off the stream will tend to take the boat out away from the jetty. The wind will assist in this and gradually your sails will fill. Using the tiller, you now steer the boat so that the wind comes over the port (left) bow. You are on the port tack. Your object is to steer the boat at an angle of roughly forty-five degrees away from the wind. The angle can be a little more than this but never less.

Remembering the rule of thumb, your sails should be trimmed to an angle of about twenty degrees from the fore-and-aft line. This means that the sheets are hauled in tight.

On this first leg you should be content to steer a course so that your sails are nicely filled with wind, and to avoid the mistake made by so many beginners of trying to sail too close to the wind. I'll consider this again in a moment.

Your first reaction, of course, is exhilaration to find the boat going ahead through the water. At last it is really happening. You also notice that the boat is heeling over to one side.

Now you will appreciate what I was discussing earlier, that intellectual stuff about two components. Besides driving you ahead, the wind in the sails is trying to push your boat sideways. This is being resisted by the boat's shape and especially by the centre-plate which is right down in the water. So the boat heels over towards the lee side.

This is all right, but don't let the boat heel over too far. Keep the lee gunwhale well clear of the water. How? Principally by your weight. You and your crew use your weight to best advantage by sitting well out on the weather side. This will come naturally anyway. Instinct will tell you both to get up on the high side away from the water.

If your weight is not enough to prevent the boat heeling too far, you can reduce the wind pressure in the sails by easing out a little on the sheets. This will spill some wind.

Now notice what happens when you move the tiller and let the boat change direction slightly. Do this very gently for the present. If you let the tiller move away from you just a little bit, the boat's bows will turn slowly towards the wind. And the luff (the leading edge) of your mainsail will start to shiver. Now pull the tiller towards you carefully; the boat's head turns away from the wind and the sails cease to shake.

This is very important and gives you valuable information. As you get more practice and experience you will learn to watch the luff of the mainsail and to steer your boat just clear of this 'shivering' course. Then you will be sailing most effectually to windward.

This will also teach you to keep 'finding' the wind. One of the greatest difficulties for beginners is the problem of wind direction. Although for the sake of simplicity I have talked of the wind coming from such and such a direction, and I shall have to continue doing so, it is a fact that even a steady breeze changes its direction slightly from time to time. This can be very puzzling.

Now, quite early, you have learned one way of watching for this. As you sail along you try with your tiller, quite gently, of course, to see when the luff is about to shiver.

There are other ways of keeping an eye on the wind's direction.

One will come with experience and has something to do with the feel of it on your cheek or the back of the neck. Another is to watch a wind pendant flown at the masthead. Some people like pieces of cotton or wool tied to the shrouds. One very good way is to learn to watch the water up to windward and study the direction of the ripples and wavelets.

The point is now obvious that on a tack like this, when you are said to be 'beating to windward', you steer your boat according to the wind's direction and not by some distant object on the shore.

And you will now realise that there is another method of spilling the wind out of your sails if you can't stop your boat heeling too far just by using your weight. This is to put your tiller down (away from you) and let the boat's bows come up towards the wind. This is called 'luffing'. It is a most useful expedient if a heavier puff of wind, a gust or a squall strikes you. Quite obviously, it serves to take the pressure off the sails. But it should be done carefully. It is essentially a temporary manoeuvre. You do not want to come right up into the wind or you'll lose your way through the water and lie helpless. In heavy weather you might then be blown over. When luffing, your aim is to get temporary relief until the gust or squall is past but not to lose the way off your boat.

You should study the feel of the tiller and how much effort

Starboard
Tack

Head to
Wind

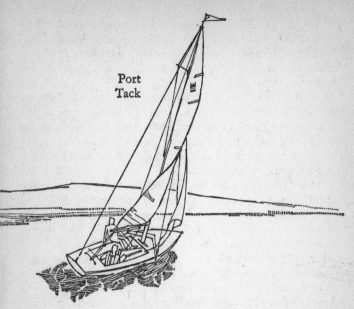

Port
Tack

Fig 7. Tacking or 'going about'

is needed to alter course; it may surprise you at first to find how little is needed to bring your boat up towards the wind and how much to 'bear away' from it.

By now you have gone far enough on this first leg on the port tack. Your next job is to go about on to the other tack. It is by a succession of these tacks with the wind on alternate sides that you make progress.

When you are ready, you can warn your crew by calling 'ready about'. This is followed by 'Lee-O' as you push the tiller towards the lee side. I use the term push but you will have discovered already that very little effort is required on the tiller to let the boat turn towards the wind. And, in fact, you ought to avoid using the tiller violently or excessively because too much rudder will act as a brake and take the way off your boat.

In most small boats with good way on them, this easy movement of the tiller is all that is required to make your boat go about. The boat answers the rudder and the bows come up into the wind, carry on past it and soon you are settled on the next tack.

Your crew allows the foresail to fly across the boat and then controls it with the other rope of the foresail sheets. The mainsail goes slack as the boat turns, the boom comes across and then is settled on the opposite side. While all this is going on you and your crew shift over to the other side, which now becomes the new weather side.

In the circumstances, the manoeuvre could not be easier. But if you have not enough speed on your boat, or if you are in a sluggish boat, you may not be able to depend on the rudder alone. You may need to help things by working the sails in the fashion described as follows.

The foresail, being before (in front of) the mast, has a tendency to pull the boat's head away from the wind. It is, of course, our old chum the sideways component cropping up again. The mainsail, on the other hand, is abaft the mast and has the opposite effect; it tends to turn the boat into the wind.

You may find this easier to understand if you recollect your experiments in a pulling-boat and how a boat pivots when it is turning. A sailing boat can be considered to be pivoting about the mast, and the effect of a sideways push on either the foresail or the mainsail will be obvious.

To assist the rudder in turning the boat into the wind, you can ease away on the foresail sheets or let them fly altogether. This clearly removes the pull away from the wind. You can also, if this is not enough, haul in on the mainsail.

As soon as your bows have passed the wind you can use your sails to help her round. The same principles are involved but now your crew holds the foresail so as to catch the wind. He may even 'back' the foresail, that is, hold it across on the wrong side for a time.

Once round on the new tack, you adjust your sails and sheets as before. Now, settled on the starboard tack, you will notice that the new course is just about at right angles to where you were steering formerly.

Before leaving the subject, let us consider what the consequences may be if you don't do the job properly. Perhaps you do not have good way on the boat when you put the tiller down. Perhaps, – and this happens so often that you may be tempted to brain him – your crew pulls the foresail across too soon.

Anyway, your boat turns sluggishly until it is pointing right into the wind. And it stops there. This situation is known as being 'in stays' and it looks ridiculous. Your sails flap ineffectually, the boat begins to drop astern and you come over all hot and bothered. The best you can do is to coax her round on to one tack or the other with the sails, with the rudder or even – and this is the end – with an oar or a paddle over the side.

Avoid this situation if you wish to retain calm nerves and enjoy sailing. Reflect on the points I have already made. Keep good way on your boat before you go about. Use your rudder moderately and work your sails if necessary. If you do the exercise properly, you will feel beautifully smug as you speed away on the new tack.

Chapter Five
Reaching

When you have had plenty of practice in beating to windward, you come to a bend in the river and you can try your hand at reaching.

You alter your course away from the wind by pulling up on the tiller. The boat's head pays off and presently the wind is coming across the beam. As you go round, you ease away the sheets, remembering our rule of thumb, until the sails are roughly forty-five degrees from the fore-and-aft line. You don't need so much lateral resistance now so your crew pulls the centre plate half-way up.

Reaching is often said to be the easiest form of sailing. Certainly it gives you more freedom. When you were beating you had to keep alert constantly in case you steered too close to the wind. You will discover later that steering can also be critical when you are running. But now, while reaching, a slight deviation from your course one way or the other is not so important. You may, if you wish, steer by some distant mark on the shore. Even so, don't get an impression that you should become casual. At all times when sailing, keep an eye to the wind's direction in case it shifts.

Let us make the most of this new-found freedom by studying a few more fine points.

You are now sailing in a direction about ninety degrees from the wind. As well as driving the boat along, the pressure in the sails is causing the boat to heel. Therefore the lee side is deeper in the water than the weather side. As the boat cleaves its way through the water, the lee bow takes more pressure than the weather bow. Consequently the boat keeps trying to turn up into the wind. To counteract this pull up on the tiller.

This is known as weather helm (you are pulling the tiller

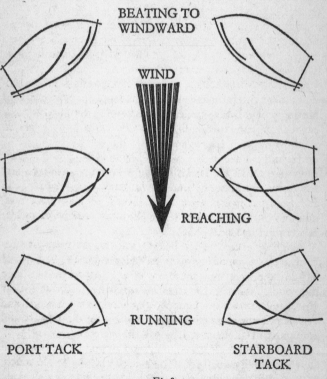

Fig 8.

up towards the weather side) and it is a sign that your boat is well trimmed. It is also a safety factor as it will help you luff into the wind quickly if you should need to. If you let go of the tiller the boat will luff up on her own.

You can adjust the amount of weather helm in various ways. One is by the trim of the sails. I have already briefly discussed the effect of the wind on the foresail and mainsail and showed how this knowledge can be used to help when going about. Consider it again while you are reaching because you now have an excellent chance to demonstrate the independent actions of each sail.

First of all, ease away (the usual order is 'check away') the foresail sheet.

Now you have reduced some of the sideways pressure before the pivoting point (the mast). Your boat will try even harder to turn up into the wind and you'll require more weather helm to counteract this tendency.

Trim the foresail again and now check away on the mainsheet. This time you have reduced some of the pressure abaft the mast. So the boat has less inclination to turn up to windward. And you will need less weather helm to keep her on course.

These experiments will help to fix in your mind the influence of each sail. And they will teach you to trim your sails to best advantage. Remember that a certain amount of weather helm is a good thing; but evidently it should not be excessive as, apart from tiring the helmsman, the extra amount of rudder in use will act as a drag in the water.

The independent action of each sail and the inter-play between them is worth studying in order to get the best out of your boat. A common tendency among beginners is to keep the foresail hauled in too taut. A moment's thought will show that this often causes a back eddy of wind on the mainsail and robs it of some of its efficiency. So keep your crew awake and lively and watch the trim of your sails at all times.

You and your crew are, of course, keeping the boat well balanced with your weight. If the heel tends to be too much, you will both be sitting out on the weather side. If this is not enough when a gust or a squall comes along, you can ease the pressure on your sails by checking out on your sheets, thereby spilling some of the wind. Then you haul them in again when the squall is past.

Every beginner should cultivate the habit of working the sheets whenever a blow comes along. Do this even to the point of exaggeration, because, for some reason, it is not an instinctive reaction.

Many a time I have seen a beginner with his teeth clenched, hanging on to a sheet when the boat has been struck by a squall, as if he were clutching grimly at some life-line. It is, as it happens, quite the wrong thing to do and often results in a capsize. One of your earliest lessons, you will recall, was to let go the sheet whenever you want to take the pressure off the sails.

Once again, be warned to keep the lee gunwale (edge of the boat) clear of the water. It looks exciting and impressive when the gunwale is skimming along close to the water but you must realise that, as a beginner, you may be rather slow at responding to the vagaries of the wind and you may not react in time to correct that extra puff. In many boats, if you let water come in over the gunwale, you'll capsize. It will not be the end of the world if that happens, but it's not the object of the exercise.

It is, anyway, a fallacy to suppose that a boat will sail faster because it is heeled well over. There may be exceptions but most boats are designed to sail best when they are pretty well upright.

Chapter Six
Running and Gybing

At last the time comes when you have to make your way back. On the stretches of river where you were beating to windward, you now have to run before the wind. With the experience gained so far, there are no problems in this to daunt you.

To go around into the running position from a reach, you pull up the tiller. You can help with the sails, if necessary. The boat's head pays off and the wind comes round to the quarter. You ease out the sheets as you go round. There is next to no lateral effect from the wind so the centre plate can be hauled right up.

One of the first things that will occur to you is that the wind seems lighter than before but you will soon realise that this is just a matter of relative speeds. Your mainsail will be nicely full of wind but your foresail may not be drawing so well because it is partly 'blanketed'.

As your course is altered further round the wind will come over the stern. You are now 'running with the wind aft'. Now your mainsail is right out on the beam. And your foresail will be almost completely 'blanketed' by the mainsail. It is hardly doing any work at all.

You don't want this sail to be wasted so a common practice is to haul it across to the other side. Then you have the mainsail out on one side with the foresail out on the other, and you are said to be 'goose-winged'. (See Fig 3.) Because the relative speed of the wind has dropped, the foresail may flap occasionally and sometimes a light spar is used to keep it out in position.

When you are more proficient at sailing you will come across boats with an extra sail, called a spinnaker, which is hoisted when the boat is running with the wind aft. But this would be an unnecessary complication for you at this stage.

Whenever you are running with the wind aft or nearly aft, keep a careful eye on the boom and mainsail. If, through a shift in its direction or an error in steering, the wind should get further round towards the wrong quarter, you will be 'sailing by the lee'. This is a bad practice. The wind may get on the wrong side of the mainsail, in which case you will experience an accidental gybe, an eventuality that can be unpleasant and even dangerous. The sail will come over with a smack and you may get clobbered with the boom. You may split the mast or strain it, carry away the rigging, or perhaps broach to and capsize: it can be an alarming experience.

All these things can happen in a jiffy, so you must watch out. It is important to guard against an accidental gybe. Firstly by careful steering and secondly by keeping an eye on the wind and your sails. If the wind is 'flukey', which means that its direction varies much and frequently, you may find it advisable to steer the boat slightly away from the intended course so that the wind is out on the quarter instead of right aft. Then later you steer off in the other direction with the wind on the other quarter. But don't overdo this. I sometimes see boats being steered diagonally down-wind, almost as though they were tacking to windward; the process looks silly.

Sometimes, and especially when there is some movement on the water, the boat develops a sort of roll, like a ship at sea. This also may lead to an accidental gybe, since the weight

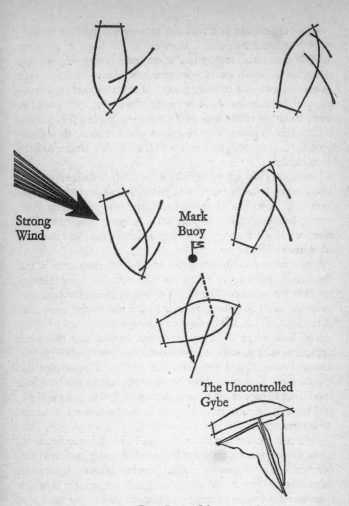

Strong
Wind

Mark
Buoy

The Uncontrolled
Gybe

Fig 9. Racing Gybes

of the boom tends to bring the sail over. A steadying hand
from your crew to keep the boom out on the proper side is
usually all that is necessary.

There are times when you may see any number of examples of an uncontrolled gybe. I am thinking of the sort of thing that happens on a blustery day when small racing dinghies are rounding a mark-buoy. Their helmsmen, generally young, are so carried away by the excitement of the race that they have no time for niceties. As they round the mark, over goes the tiller, round goes the boat and – wham! – the sail flies across. If they remain afloat, they've gained much time on their competitors. If not, well, they can wait for the club tender to help them back.

Don't confuse an accidental gybe with a deliberate one. The former is nasty because it generally catches you by surprise. The latter is a prefectly legitimate way of altering your course because you will pick your moment and control it. Even so, it is a tactic to be conducted with care and avoided altogether in heavy weather.

To perform a deliberate gybe, you take up any slack in the mainsheet, then haul it in steadily while you put your tiller up towards the weather side. In my opinion, this is the best moment for you and your crew to move across to the other side of the boat, which will be the new weather side.

The boat turns in response to the rudder and the wind draws round the stern of the boat. You are hauling in the mainsail steadily and presently the wind will blow into the reverse side. The sail and boom are blown across the boat and you let the sheet run out to ease the strain. Just as this happens, you reverse the tiller smartly to stop the boat clawing up towards the wind.

This last instruction is most important. To emphasise it, let us reflect upon a characteristic of all floating craft that has worried sailors through the ages. Vessels running before the wind have a strong tendency to 'broach to', which is to say that they are liable, especially in heavy weather, to turn violently round towards the wind. When they reach a course where the wind comes over the beam they may capsize. Many a sailing ship was lost or dismasted in this way.

In our small boat we have already seen that, when we are beating to windward or reaching, the pressures of the water

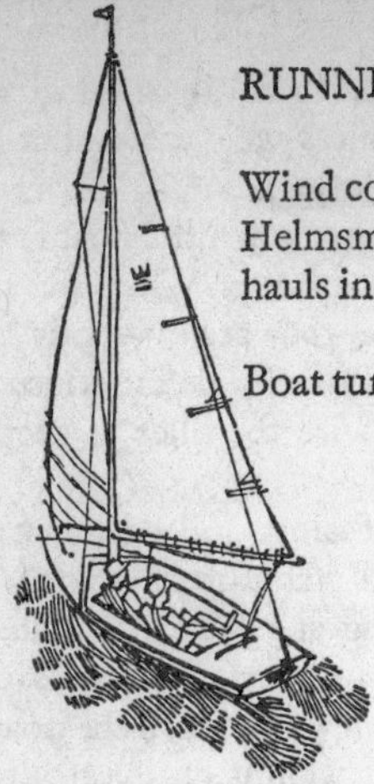

RUNNING FREE TO PORT

Wind coming over port quarter.
Helmsman pulls up tiller and
hauls in main sheet.

Boat turns away from wind.

STERN TO WIND

Helmsman and crew
change sides.

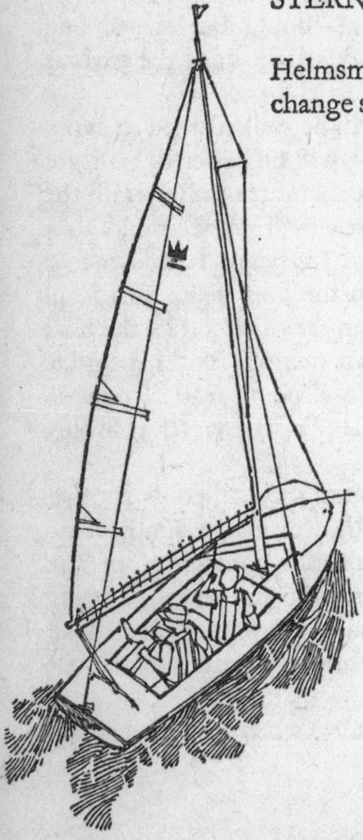

RUNNING FREE
TO STARBOARD

Wind comes on to starboard
quarter. Helmsman lets
main sheet run out and
reverses tiller (to prevent
boat 'broaching to').

When boat is steady, Helmsman
trims sheets and resumes
normal steering.

Fig 10. The Gybe (controlled)

on the deeper lee side and of the wind in the mainsail will cause us to luff into the wind unless we use weather helm to keep the boat on course.

These pressures are even stronger when the boat is running with the wind coming over the quarter. When the mainsail blows across the boat as we gybe, they are evidently stronger still. In any sort of wind you will feel a definite lurch. It requires early and decisive action with the tiller to keep out of trouble.

All this may seem rather confusing. Indeed when you do it for the first few times, you will get a pretty strong impression that everything is happening at once. It is quite on the cards that you will even be unsure which way you are going. This is why I advise you to change your side in the boat before the gybe gets started. Also, your weight on the new weather side is useful when the boat lurches to the pull of the sail.

Needless to say, the manoeuvre should be learned and practised frequently while the wind is light until the various movements become automatic.

When the wind is strong, you will be well advised to avoid the gybe. To alter your direction it will be better to go right round the other way. For instance, if you are sailing with the wind on the starboard quarter, you will come round to a reach and then to the close-hauled starboard tack. Up into the wind and about, to pay off on the port tack. This is all safe enough so far. Now you pull up the tiller and let the boat pay off until the wind is on the port quarter. You have gone around through three-quarters of a circle instead of one, so it may take a little longer, but it may be well worth it if only for your peace of mind.

Before I leave the subject of running free, there is another point you should be reminded about. Remember you have no brakes. You can't pull the communication cord and stop. You must keep a sharp look-out for some distance ahead, bearing in mind that the only method to take the way off your boat, short of lowering the sails, is to bring her around into the wind.

This is what you will do, naturally, when you get back to

your berth. You will not attempt to go alongside while you have the wind and stream behind you. When you are abreast of your berth, you will turn your boat around and fetch up alongside, head to wind. Get your painter ashore and then lower the sails.

Chapter Seven
Rule of the Road

In many ways it is a pity that the beginner cannot sail displaying L-plates. As it is, boats are liable to come at you from many directions and, unless your newness to the sport is painfully obvious, all will expect you to take appropriate action to avoid collision.

For your first trip I crossed my fingers and hoped that all would be for the best. In any case this was one reason why I advised you to start on a quiet river. But you cannot postpone study of what is required when you encounter other craft.

When you are riding a bicycle or driving a car along the highways, you have a fairly simple set of rules, the principle being that you should keep to the correct side of the road. In this country it is the left-hand side and oncoming traffic passes on your right.

On the rivers, in estuaries and in narrow channels, as it happens, the 'working side' is the right-hand or starboard side and if you are in a pulling-boat or a power-boat this must always be borne in mind.

In a sailing boat, things are not so simple. As you know by

now, you cannot, as a rule, steer straight along a river; you have to be continually dodging one way or the other as the wind dictates. And so, of course, do the other sailing boats you meet. If there were not clear rules as to the conduct of craft under various circumstances, a right royal chaos would ensue.

There is a set of regulations which have come down to us (with amendments) from the days of sailing ships to govern the behaviour of almost everything that floats. They are the International Regulations for Preventing Collisions at Sea and are popularly referred to as 'The Rule of the Road at Sea'. Professional sailors have to know them thoroughly but you in your small sailing boat will get by with a good grasp of a few essentials.

Generally speaking, the regulations require that when two vessels (craft or boats) are approaching one another so that there might be a collision if they held their courses, one vessel must take the requisite action to keep clear while the other continues on her way. And each should know what the other is expected to do.

You can see the sense of this. It might be just as disastrous if both tried to keep clear, as if both ignored the other.

It is a general principle that steamers (which means all vessels being driven by power, even if they also have sails up) keep out of the way of sailing vessels. Most people seem to know this; but don't be misled by it.

You are not allowed, for instance, to block a fairway. I heard of a chap sailing over from the Solent who thought a large liner coming down Southampton Water ought to stop to let him pass across to the Hamble! The Harbour-master's launch corrected him.

On a river you may encounter launches which have to keep to a schedule and local bye-laws may require you not to delay them. Large steamers run the risk of going aground if they stop in a narrow channel. Anyway, such vessels probably have less manoeuvrability than you have. So, naturally, you must use your common sense.

In this book, we are mainly concerned with what happens

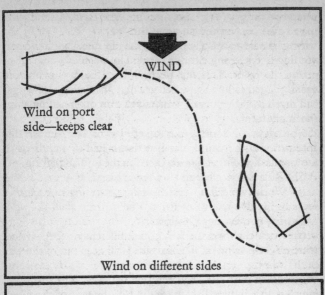

Wind on port
side—keeps clear

WIND

Wind on different sides

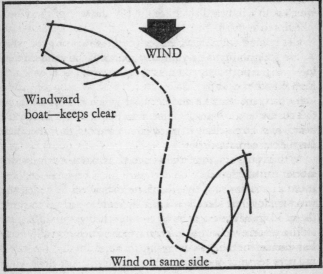

Windward
boat—keeps clear

WIND

Wind on same side

Fig 11. Rule of the Road

when two sailing vessels are meeting. And the rules in this respect have been very much simplified.

After the best part of a century, the old rule – about vessels running free keeping clear of vessels close-hauled – was dropped in the 1960s. This rule derived from the days of the old square-rigged sailing ships, when a close-hauled square-rigger had much less freedom of manoeuvre than other sailing ships she might meet.

Nowadays of course, the square-rigger has almost disappeared and the world of sail is dominated by hundreds of thousands of yachts and boats carrying the fore-and-aft rig.

The Rule is now clear and is worded like this : –

(a) When two sailing vessels are approaching one another so as to involve risk of collision, one of them shall keep out of the way of the other as follows : –

(i) When each has the wind on a different side, the vessel which has the wind on the port side shall keep out of the way of the other.

(ii) When both have the wind on the same side, the vessel which is to windward shall keep out of the way of the vessel which is to leeward.

Just remind yourself whenever you go about or gybe what your responsibility is on your new course. If the wind is coming over the port side, you must keep clear of any boat which is on the other tack.

If you come up with another boat which has the wind on the same side as yourself, remember that it is the windward boat which keeps clear. In many circumstances, the other boat may be close to a 'lee-shore'.

As this is the first time we have come across this expression, a brief explanation may be necessary for a beginner. A 'lee-shore' is a shore or a river bank or a shoal on to which the wind is blowing; since it is more difficult to sail up towards the wind (it has to be done by tacking this way and that) no sailing vessel ever wishes to get too close. Such a position was a nightmare for the old sailing ship masters.

There remains one more rule to which I must draw your attention because the regulations are emphatic about it. The wording is 'Notwithstanding anything contained in these rules, every vessel overtaking any other shall keep out of the way of the overtaken vessel.'

If, one day, your dream should come true and you should find yourself in your sailing vessel rapidly overtaking a smart 'gin palace' crawling back home with engine trouble, remember it's your job to keep clear!

Chapter Eight
'Phase Two': Boats

So far my purpose has been to encourage you to get into a boat and do the right things under simple, easy conditions. I have injected a little theory now and then, but practice and experience are the most important parts of the prescription.

Those first few trips under sail will have taught you the elementary tricks of keeping your boat moving by the wind's force. You will have learned the feel of the tiller, the response of the boat to gusts and squalls, the effect of shifting your weight and dozens of other wrinkles about sheets and sails which can't be picked up merely by reading a book.

But you still have plenty to learn so don't make the mistake of being rash and over-confident. Let the tortoise rather than the hare be the symbol of your progress.

What you have done so far has been 'Phase One' of your training. It should have been enough to show you the pleasures of sailing and to stimulate your enthusiasm. You are ready now to advance to the next phase; to acquire a more comprehensive knowledge of boats, their characteristics and their performance.

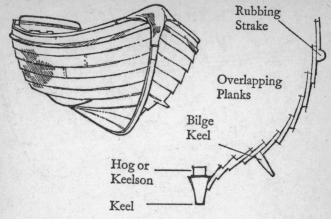

Fig 12. Clinker Built

In the endless variety of small boats, you will soon become aware of distinctive types of construction.

You will see the 'clinker-built' boat, in which the planking runs in a fore-and-aft direction with each plank overlapping the one beneath. It is an easily recognised feature.

This type of construction makes a strong boat and repairs are fairly straightforward since a damaged plank may be taken out and replaced without having to dismantle a large part of the boat. This method of construction has been in regular use in the Royal and Merchant Navies for years for some of the heaviest and largest boats. It is also favoured for many popular racing dinghies.

You will also see the 'carvel-built' boat, in which the planks are fitted edge to edge to form a flush surface. This type of construction appeals strongly to yachtsmen since the smooth sides simply scream for glossy paints and varnishes. Some builders achieve the carvel-built finish by shaping and glueing together laminates of thin wood around a mould. The method produces a tough and handsome boat.

In modern times fibre glass has come steadily into the picture. Boats of this kind, also, are made by means of moulds.

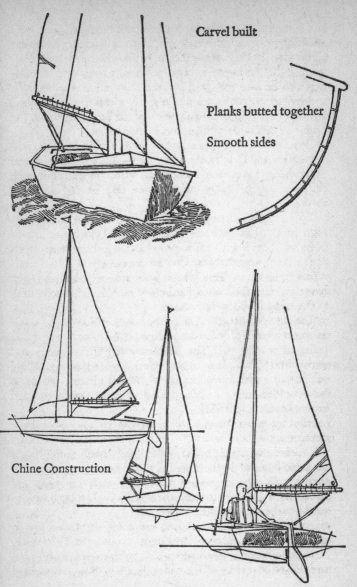

Carvel built

Planks butted together

Smooth sides

Chine Construction

Fig 13. Carvel and Chine

In the early days there were doubts about them and there were 'teething troubles' with early models mainly on account of the resins used, but nowadays they have proved themselves. They make light, strong and very satisfactory craft and there is much to be said for them because they reduce maintenance and repair problems to a minimum. But it is too early to say whether they will eventually achieve the long life which has been a remarkable feature of some wooden boats.

Other materials are occasionally used to make boats; aluminium alloy and light steel plating are sometimes met with and experiments have even been made with concrete, but such craft are comparatively rare and you may never run across them.

You will find distinctive features in the shape of boats. A high proportion have the rounded bilge which has always been associated with sailing vessels. In others there is an angled joint near the waterline, where rather flat sides meet a rather flat bottom. This joint is known as a 'chine' and such boats are described as of hard chine or soft chine according to the angle at which they are set.

The chine construction helps the boat to plane on the water as speed increases. It has also helped constructors who build boats of marine ply. The problems of putting bends and curves into plywood are largely avoided when it is used. Many of the firms which produce do-it-yourself kits for the home boat builders rely on this method of construction to keep their customers satisfied.

Another distinction you will observe is that some boats have decking and others have not. The latter are called 'open' boats and include nearly all pulling-craft. Many small sailing boats are open boats and others are only partly decked. This partial deck usually amounts to a foredeck and small side decks and these obviously help to keep the boat dry when beating into a head sea or when heeling to a squall.

You will already have noticed that some boats seem low in the water while others are floating high out of it. This brings us to the subject of freeboard which, in simple parlance is the amount of boat clear of the water. Boats with high freeboard

Trimmed by the stern
(and overloaded!)

Trimmed by the head

Fig 14. Trim

have a lot of dry side; boats with low freeboard have their gunwales close to the surface.

Freeboard varies according to the weight of the boat and the load it is carrying and it indicates the amount of reserve buoyancy. A merchant ship with no cargo aboard may have a high freeboard of, say, twenty or thirty feet. She then has a lot of reserve buoyancy. When fully loaded with a heavy cargo she goes down in the water and may have only ten feet or so of freeboard. She then has much less reserve buoyancy. The subject is not merely academic. Small boats are sometimes overloaded until they have only a few inches of freeboard and this can cause accidents.

Observe a small boat floating on the water and take a note of its freeboard. Now see what happens when a man goes aboard and sits in the middle. There is a slight decrease in freeboard throughout the length of the boat.

Ask him to move forward and sit in the forward end of the boat and note how the bows sink lower while the stern rises. Now the boat is said to be 'trimmed by the head'. Ask him to move right aft and note how the stern goes down and the bows rise. Now the boat is 'trimmed by the stern'.

I do not suggest these experiments merely to indicate what is obvious. The trim of a boat is important to its performance whether it is under oars or sail or power.

You can prove for yourself that a boat under oars is far more difficult to steer when it is trimmed by the head than when 'on an even keel' or trimmed by the stern. Now consider the effect of trim on your sailing boat. Consider a wind blowing across the beam and neglect for a moment the effect on the sails.

If the boat is trimmed by the head, the tendency is for the stern to blow away from the wind because the bows are taking more water resistance. The boat will try to turn until it is pointing into the wind. Therefore you need more weather helm.

Conversely, if the boat is trimmed by the stern, the bows tend to blow away from the wind and you need little or no weather helm. You may even be carrying lee helm, which is a bad thing. Clearly, all this will be important when you want to get the best out of the boat. By shifting weight, which is to say, moving yourself and your crew, even a short distance towards the bows or the stern, you can improve the trim and get better performance and speed. A rather extreme instance of this came to my notice some time ago.

A very useful class of fibre glass sailing boat had been produced by the Admiralty for training cadets and I heard it stated that these boats were not much use as they would not sail to windward. But the true cause was that instructors were putting too many trainees on the after and midship thwarts, and the boats were trimmed too much by the stern. When these boats are properly trimmed, their performance to windward is excellent.

Now let us move on to another important aspect of the behaviour of boats, namely, stability. A ship or a boat is designed and built to float upright and when water or the wind pushes the boat momentarily over to one side, the natural reaction is for it to roll back to the upright position.

This can all be explained by discourses on centres of gravity, centres of buoyancy, metacentres and so on, but you need not become so involved.

It is enough to be satisfied that the boat which returns to the upright position promptly is a stable boat. If it doesn't, or if it carries on turning and capsizes, it is unstable. In a small boat, this latter condition can be achieved by bad loading or through ignorance.

The weight to be considered is usually that of the people in the boat. You have seen that a boat must not be overloaded to the extent that the freeboard becomes too little. You must now realise that the weight in a boat should be kept down low. In other words, the occupants of a boat should not stand up. When they do so they raise the centre of gravity and make the craft unstable.

It is a good general rule to keep your crew and passengers seated on the thwarts; in certain circumstances you may have to be even more cautious and have them lower still, on the bottom boards.

The stability of a sailing boat is most important and involves some interesting points. In the first place you have the extra top weight of mast and spars and sails carried high above the boat. Furthermore you have wind pressure in the sails trying to blow the boat over.

Large racing yachts usually have heavy, deep keels to compensate for top weight and to improve their sailing qualities. Commercial and ex-commercial sailing vessels and craft which operate in shallow waters cannot accept these deep keels so their compensation usually is in the form of ballast or cargo, and their sailing qualities, which might be impaired by flat keels, are assisted sometimes by lee-boards. These two boards are carried on either side and one is lowered when on a tack to increase the lateral resistance in the water.

These various considerations affect the design of small boats. Most small boats are provided with a centre plate. (This is sometimes called a drop-keel but the term is inaccurate. A drop-keel was fitted in early submarines; it could be released if the submarine was in difficulties and struggling to surface).

The centre-plate is housed in a box-like structure sticking up in the middle of the boat. This box encloses a hole through the bottom of the boat and must therefore extend above the water-line to prevent the boat filling up. The centre-plate is hinged inside this box and can be raised or lowered as required, by hand, by a winch or some kind of tackle.

When the centre-plate is housed in its box the draught of the boat will be small and she may be navigated across shallow patches with ease. If she sits in the mud at low water in harbour, there are no problems. But when the centre-plate is fully lowered, the draught may be increased by three or four feet, so you will have to be careful where you go.

Originally, the centre-plate was a good heavy steel plate which performed useful functions. It did, of course, provide lateral resistance in the water, which is essential if the boat is going to sail properly on a beat or a reach.

Being heavy, it also provided very useful weight low down; it lowered the centre of gravity, gave valuable compensation for all the top hamper, and was an important aid to the boat's stability.

Nowadays, however, a fashion has crept in of providing wooden centre-plates. These, like the lee-boards of larger craft, give the lateral resistance which is necessary for sailing, but they provide no weight below.

In my opinion this is a pity, because the action of the centre-plate in providing lateral resistance can, in itself contribute to capsizing. When one considers that the pressure on the sails (high up) is trying to push the boat sideways, and the resist-

Yacht Keel

Lee-board

Centre plate

Fig 15. Keels

ance of the centre-plate (low down) is a force in the opposite direction, you will see that there is a definite couple most favourable to a capsize. This is manageable when the plate is heavy and gives extra stability but when it does not it imperils the craft. Avoiding the capsize depends on the agility of the crew.

We have one more characteristic to discuss before I pass on from the fascinating study of boats. It is buoyancy. Without it, the other characteristics couldn't exist.

If a boat is holed, its natural buoyancy is lost as it fills with water. A wooden boat may not sink but it will become 'awash' and your tenancy on board will become uncomfortable. In some instances, particularly when there is solid ballast aboard, a wooden boat will sink.

To allow for such contingencies and ensure a sporting chance of saving the boat, it is common practice nowadays to fit additional buoyancy apparatus. This may take the form of copper tanks fitted under thwarts and benches, patent plastic material built into lockers and compartments, or air bags which are blown up and secured in convenient positions. If the boat is holed or capsized this extra buoyancy will help to keep it floating well out of the water.

If the crew in addition are wearing lifejackets and are themselves well supported in the water, they have a good chance of salvaging the vessel.

Chapter Nine

Masts, Spars and Sails

From the study of boats we come naturally to a survey of the gear used to propel them.

Most small sailing boats have only one mast, which is 'stepped' in place about one quarter or one third of the boat's length from forward. It is usually made of wood, although aluminium masts are becoming more common.

The mast may be stepped in the hog or keelson or on the foredeck. Sometimes it is hinged in a sort of box called a 'tabernacle'. Often there is an arrangement for clamping the mast in its erect position, and in most cases it is supported also by 'standing rigging'.

A simple form of standing rigging consists of a forestay leading up from the stem-post and two shrouds one each side, from the gunwales abreast the mast. (See fig 5.) The forestay supports it from forward and is especially useful when the mast is carrying the weight of the mainsail and its spars. The shrouds give athwartship support and come into play especially when the boat is heeling. The thrust from the sails has also to be considered, of course.

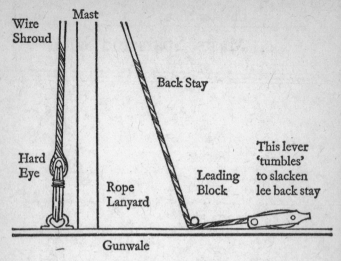

Fig 16. Shrouds and Backstays

In some boats, usually the larger types, provision is also made to support the mast from aft. This is not easy because the mainsail is in the way. One method is to fit a pair of back stays aft of the shrouds; the one on the leeward side has to be slacked away or let go whenever the mainsail would foul it. This can be difficult for an inexperienced crew when the boat is running and gybing.

As a general rule, the standing rigging is made of wire rope which is set up taut by lanyards or slips and bottle-screws.

One of the oldest of sailing rigs is the lateen sail which is still extensively used in many parts of the world. The feluccas of Egypt and the dhows and prows of the Indian Ocean are probably the best known examples.

In single-masted vessels, the lateen sail is a huge piece of canvas, nearly triangular in shape, suspended from a very long yard and this yard is partially balanced, slung and hauled up the mast. The sail extends before the mast as well as abaft it and circus performers have nothing on agile native sailors

Sets beautifully
on Leeside of
mast

Not so good when
yard is on
weather side.

Fig 17. The Lateen Sail

when they sprint up and down this yard setting the sail or gathering it in.

The rig probably owes its long survival to its simplicity and the fact that in those parts of the world sailors can generally rely on steady winds, the direction of the wind being determined by monsoons or other seasonal factors.

The sail sets beautifully when the yard is on the lee side of the mast but it loses some efficiency if the yard is on the weather side, when the sail is distorted by the mast. The yard

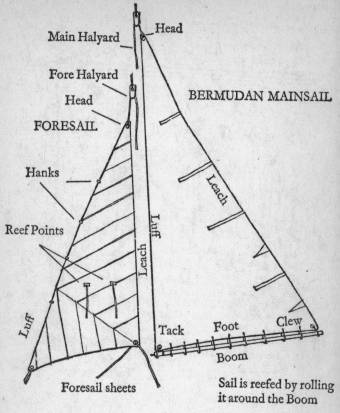

Main Halyard — Head

Fore Halyard

Head

FORESAIL

BERMUDAN MAINSAIL

Hanks

Leach

Reef Points

Luff

Leach

Luff

Tack   Foot   Clew

Boom

Foresail sheets

Sail is reefed by rolling
it around the Boom

Fig 18

can be dipped or shifted to the other side, but the normal practice of these sailors is to set the yard on the lee side for what will be their long working tack. In the case of the dhows this may last them for days on end.

Short legs on the other tack, which may be necessary to manoeuvre in and out of harbour, are accepted without moving the yard across.

Somewhere and sometime it occurred to someone that this

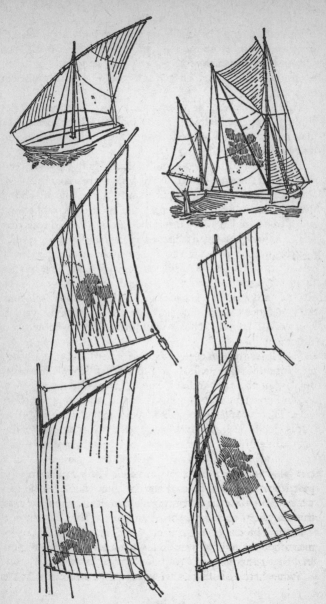

Fig 19. Sails

complication could be avoided by having two sails instead of one; a foresail before the mast and a mainsail abaft it. Then the mast would never get in the way; the sails could cross the boat quite easily for either tack and would be equally efficient on either side.

This is the pattern for most modern rigs. The foresail varies slightly but, essentially, it is a triangular sail set before the mast and controlled by the fore sheets. The mainsail comes in many versions. (See fig. 19.)

The nearest to the lateen sail is the lugsail. This is a rectangular sail suspended from a yard which is partially balanced, slung and hoisted up the mast. A small part of this sail and of the yard extends before the mast, not by design but because it can't be avoided. Very often the yard is attached to a ring (called a traveller) which is hauled up the mast by the halyard.

The traveller is secured to the yard about one quarter or one third of its length from the forward end. The further along the yard the traveller is attached, the easier it will be to dip the yard around the mast; this is usually done each time the boat goes about onto the other tack so that the yard is kept on the lee side. This is why this version is known as a 'dipping lug'.

The closer the traveller is to the forward end of the yard, the more difficult it will be to dip the yard round the mast. But less of the yard and sail extend before the mast so it is not so important and dipping is not usually done for short tacks. This version is known as a 'standing lug'.

It is clearly desirable to do away with any protrusion of the mainsail before the mast and this can be achieved by a gaff rig. The mainsail in this rig is hoisted on a gaff, which is a spar fitted with jaws on its forward end. The jaws slide up the mast when the sail is hoisted and keep the whole of the gaff and sail abaft the mast. It is normally necessary to have two main halyards, one at the throat and one at the peak, or else a system of blocks.

Another method of hoisting a mainsail with all its area abaft the mast is to use a sprit boom; a spar extending diagonally across the sail from the tack to its peak. This was a favourite method with the old Thames sailing barges, but is seldom used in small boats.

Experience has shown that a mainsail performs better up to windward when it has a long leading edge. The analogy of the aeroplane's wing has already been mentioned. Consequently two other rigs have now become very common. The gunter rig is one of them and it is an improvement on the gaff rig. The gunter yard has a fitting at its forward end (called the throat), somewhat similar to the gaff jaws and when the sail is hoisted the yard is peaked right up until it is nearly vertical. It then becomes virtually an extension of the mast. This obviously gives a long leading edge to the sail. There are however, objections to carrying this long gunter yard. It means a lot of extra weight carried high above the boat. So the Bermudan rig has become more and more fashionable, particularly in racing craft.

In this, the boat is fitted with a mast long enough to take all of the luff of a triangular mainsail. Now you have a rig of many virtues, no heavy spars up aloft and a long leading edge giving maximum efficiency to the sail; an easy mainsail to hoist and to stow away.

The beginner may reasonably ask why all boats are not fitted with this Bermudan rig and there are several answers. The very long mast can be a nuisance, particularly in a cruising boat. Before sailing under bridges, the lot may have to be taken down. When not in use the mast is too long to be stowed. Usually it is left in position and this may lead to trouble, especially if it is the practice to keep the boat lying at a buoy. A boat with a Bermudan mast used to lie at the next buoy to my gunter-rigged cruiser. After a gale it was not unusual to find she had been blown over by the force of the wind on her high mast.

A consideration of these factors may help when you decide to buy your own boat. As you can see, much depends on the sort of sailing you want to take up and the locality in which you want to do it.

One other spar which I must briefly discuss is the boom. This keeps the foot of the sail stretched and spreads the main-

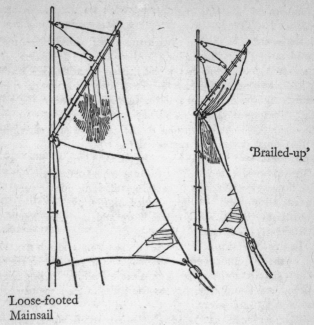

'Brailed-up'

Loose-footed
Mainsail

Fig 20. Brails

sail to the best advantage. It enables one to trim the sail at its
best angle to the wind. The forward end of the boom usually
is held to the mast by a 'gooseneck' while the after end is controlled by the mainsheet.

Even the boom is not completely free of criticism. One of
its disadvantages is that the sail cannot be 'brailed-up'. This
is a useful method by which a loose-footed sail can be gathered
into the mast quickly and thereby spilled of wind. There is
also a risk that the boom when out on the beam will dip into
the water when the boat rolls or when she is caught by a heavy
squall; if this happens, life becomes hectic because it is no
longer possible to steer with the rudder. On the whole, however, these disadvantages are worth accepting because of the
extra efficiency of the sail.

We will now consider the sails which are spread on these spars. Through the ages they have been made from canvas manufactured from flax or cotton. Nowadays man-made fibres have come into the picture and the use of Terylene sails has been increasing rapidly. Practically all sails are strengthened by having what is called bolt-rope sewn along some of their edges. Incidentally, it has been long-standing British practice to sew the bolt-rope on the port side of fore and aft sails. This can be a help when unfurling a large sail and getting it bent on.

The foresail is triangular in shape and slides up and down the forestay on hanks fitted to its luff. (See fig 18.) The head of the sail is hoisted by the fore halyard; the tack is laced or shackled to the stem post and the clew is controlled by the fore sheets. Some foresails can be rolled up like cotton on a reel, around the luff. Others have rows of reef points which I will discuss later.

Your mainsail will also be triangular if you have Bermudan rig, otherwise it will be rectangular. In the latter case the head of the sail (the upper edge) will be laced to a yard, gaff or gunter yard; the luff will be laced to the mast and the foot laced to a boom. (Sometimes there are modifications, for instance, tracks in which the sails slide instead of lacing). The mainsail may have rows of reef points or it will have to be reefed by rolling it around the boom. (See fig 21.)

It is important that you should know how to reef a sail and how to shake a reef out. If you don't know the proper way you may tear the sail and ruin it, or at the very least, may spoil its shape. Whatever boat you have, the method of reefing is one of the earliest peculiarities you must study. You should practise the method, to begin with, while your boat is still in its berth. It is more difficult and may become more urgent, when you are under way.

Reefing, as you know, is the normal method of reducing the effective sail area when the wind becomes too strong. When it can be done by rolling the sail around the boom or around patent rolling gear, there is not much to it.

But if the sail is fitted with rows of reef points you must be

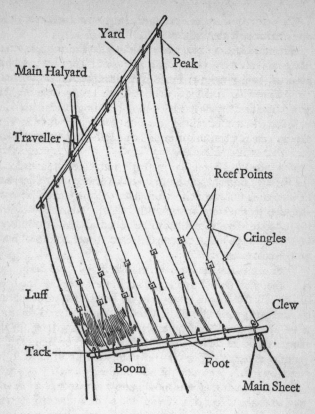

Fig 21. Reefs

careful. To put in a reef, first slacken the halyards. You will notice that on the edges of the sail (the luff and the leach) in line with the reef-points there are rings known as 'cringles', sewn into the bolt-rope. (See fig 21.) You haul these down first and lash them to the boom or the foot of the sail. Then you fold the slack of the sail in neat tucks and secure them by passing the reef points. It is hardly necessary to say that reef points are tied with reef knots.

Conversely, to shake out a reef, let go the reef-points first and then release the cringles.

The sense behind this procedure is that the biggest strain always is taken by the cringles and that means by the bolt-ropes. If you got the drill wrong and let the reef points hold the tucks of the sail by themselves, you can readily see that you might rip the sail.

When the wind is very strong, you may well need two or three reefs. The procedure is the same, but you should put the reefs in one at a time. You can shake them out in turn as the wind eases.

Try also to keep your sails balanced. By which I mean, don't put all your reefs in the mainsail with none in the fore-sail, or your boat won't sail well.

And if you have been sailing with reefed sails, don't forget to shake out the reefs before you stow away the sails; then you won't spoil their shape.

Chapter Ten
Ropes and Ropework

Every small boat sailor must have some facility with ropes and ropework.

There are two main types, wire rope and fibre rope. In small boats the former will not amount to much. The biggest items of wire rope in your boat will be the stays and shrouds (the standing rigging) and, as the name implies, they have little movement and most of the time stay put. Wire rope is strong and durable. From time to time, say, at the beginning of the season, it must be renewed but otherwise there isn't much to do about it.

There is no point in wasting time at this stage with a description of how to splice wire rope. Firstly because while the job is not difficult, skill comes with practice and cannot be learned from a book even with the most elaborate sketches. There is a knack in making the tucks without crippling the wire and if you wish to learn it, you had best get hold of an old sea-dog or a dockyard rigger for practical instruction.

Secondly, because you can waste a lot of expensive material

if you tackle the job without the requisite skill, and a poorly made splice will be unreliable anyway.

And finally, because the practice of splicing wire ropes in the old way is dying. Nowadays there is a splendid neat and quick method (the Talurit splice) of putting eyes in wire rope, and most firms can have this done whenever you buy new rigging.

A positive approach however, must be taken to fibre ropes. This is a fascinating skill and there is plenty to learn about it. Halyards, sheets, topping lifts, lacing, lanyards, painters and so on are all made of fibre rope. Any job which requires a rope that is flexible and easy to handle but which does not involve too much chafe is usually given to a fibre rope rather than a wire rope.

These ropes, otherwise known as cordage, are made of vegetable fibres such as coir, hemp, sisal or manilla or of man-made fibres, such as nylon. During the process of rope-making, the fibres are spun into yarns; the yarns are twisted into strands and three or four strands are made up into a rope. In most cases you will find that three strands which have been given a left-hand twist, have been made up into a rope with a right-handed lay.

This process gives to the rope its elasticity and strength. It also dictates a practice you must learn from the start. A right-handed rope should always be coiled in a right-handed (clockwise) manner otherwise it may become snarled up when you need it.

A rope's size, like a lady's waist, is normally described by the measurement of its circumference in inches; and its length in fathoms. A fathom is six feet and the sailor measures off rope by holding his arms outstretched with the rope across his chest.

The strength of a rope made of manilla, sisal or hemp can be found approximately by squaring its size (the circumference in inches) and dividing by three. This gives the breaking strains in tons. The working load then is found by dividing this by 6. Take, as an example a three-inch hemp rope. The square of 3 is 9. Dividing by 3 gives 3 tons breaking strain.

Lay first end of twine along rope.

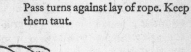

Pass turns against lay of rope. Keep
them taut.

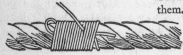

Make last half-dozen turns loosely.
Tuck last end of twine through
them.

Work all turns taut and pull last end
through.

PALM AND NEEDLE WHIPPING

Using a palm, start by passing needle
and twine through a strand.
Make all turns against the lay.

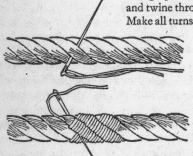

Secure turns by needling through
strands above and below them.
Keep crossing in the lays.
Finish off with half hitches in crossing.

Fig 22. Whipping

Dividing again by 6 gives a working load of half a ton. It should also be borne in mind that bends and hitches in a rope reduce the strength by about half.

Coir rope, sometimes called grass rope, is seldom used in a boat, but it has its uses in a yacht club or boat basin because it floats. It is very rough and of the same colour and material as coconut matting. You should remember that it is much weaker than the other ropes.

Nylon rope, on the other hand, is much stronger and is coming into increasing use in the yachting world. You must refer to the maker's tables to ascertain their breaking strains.

One of the first things to remember in the use and care of rope is that when it is cut, the ends will tend to unlay.

If this is neglected, you will waste much rope. It can be prevented by whippings of which there are many varieties. Two kinds will be enough for you to learn, the common whipping, which can be put on quickly, and the palm and needle whipping, which is more permanent. (See fig 22.) It is a good habit to put two whippings on the end of a rope, several inches apart, in case one comes off.

Another method of preventing a rope's end from unlaying is to put in a back-splice or an eye-splice. This is a useful dodge when in a hurry but it can't be used if the rope has to pass through a block.

Frequently it will be necessary to put an eye-splice in a rope, either with a thimble (a hard eye) or without (a soft eye), and you should learn to do this quickly and surely. The process is simple and it is a must for the small boat sailor.

You should next learn to make a short splice which is used for joining a rope that has parted or two lengths of rope of the same size. A short splice will not pass through a block and, therefore, you should also learn the long splice which will. But these are skills you will acquire more out of interest than from frequent necessity.

The quickest way of joining a rope that has parted or of joining together two ropes is by using a bend or hitch. There are many versions of these, each designed for a different purpose, mostly with the aim of being easy to make and easy to

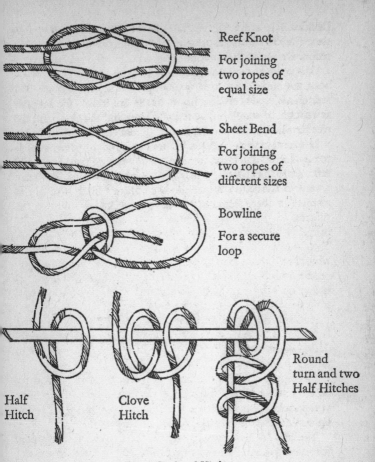

Reef Knot

For joining
two ropes of
equal size

Sheet Bend

For joining
two ropes of
different sizes

Bowline

For a secure
loop

Half
Hitch

Clove
Hitch

Round
turn and two
Half Hitches

Fig 23. Bends and Hitches

let go when the time comes. A bend or hitch which jams
when pulled tight or when rope is wet is a bad one. (See fig 23.)

Purely as a matter of interest you should note that the terms
used have been 'bends and hitches' for what a landlubber
classifies as knots. At sea, most knots are fanciful affairs, employed often for decorative as well as useful purposes. One

delightful example is the 'Double Matthew Walker' which was used in the dead-eyes of the rigging of the old sailing ships. One can't help wondering who Matthew Walker was and how the knot came to be named after him.

In the old sailing ships, which were at sea for months at a stretch and spent endless hours in the doldrums, the mariner lived a life of watch on, watch off. Time and the clock and the calendar had a meaning for him, different from what we know today. You have neither the leisure nor, probably, the patience to develop so much fondness for manipulating rope as the old sailors did. But don't, whatever you do, continue in a state where you have to ask somebody to make a hitch here or put a splice in there because you have neglected a study of the subject.

Chapter Eleven
Tide and Stream Problems

By this time the reader has already formed ideas as to the sort of sailing he will favour most. It may be dinghy racing. If so, I can give no better advice than to join a good yacht club. I can't recommend a method of winning races any more than I can pick the winner of the Grand National. But the skills acquired from regular club competition are invaluable.

Joining a club will mean that, in due course, you will wish to buy a boat of the racing class. Be a little circumspect about this. Don't buy any old second-hand boat you may come across. In racing there are pretty tight regulations about weight, dimensions, buoyancy, cut of sails and so on and if a boat doesn't conform to the rules, it will not qualify for racing. Then your money will be wasted. If in doubt ask a club member for advice.

On the other hand, you may agree with me that cruising under sail offers plenty in the way of peace and pleasure. In this case there are many hints which will be useful.

A little reminiscence on that first trip of yours will not come amiss. You learned many good lessons but it is fairly certain that you were too busy and preoccupied to pay attention to subtleties.

When you were getting ready the boat was lying alongside a jetty, head to wind and stream. To hoist the sails and get under way was simple. But, supposing the wind had been coming from the opposite direction? The operation would have been more perplexing.

Generally speaking, the wind's direction is a more decisive factor than the direction of the stream, because, as you now know, it is difficult and perhaps impossible to get the mainsail up properly unless the craft is head to wind. The answer in this case would be to turn the boat round, hold her in position with the painter and stern-fast and then get the sails up. That the boat now points downstream is just too bad and can't be helped. Anyway, with the wind in your sails, you can counteract the effect of the stream when you shove off.

You will recollect that you set off up river against the stream. As it happened, the wind was also against you and you spent a lot of time beating to windward. It was a lengthy process to cover much distance up river but you scarcely noticed it for time flies swiftly when you are sailing.

All was well. When the time came for you to turn back, you were nicely placed. Being up wind, you could run for home, a much quicker business than beating to windward. You also had the stream in your favour, so even if the wind had dropped away, you could still have made it. But if you had set off in the other direction, you would have returned battling against wind and stream and might have been very late getting back to your berth.

Which direction to choose is not always such a straightforward issue but the point is that excursions under sail should always be planned and not be haphazardly undertaken. I know of many yachtsmen who have spent hours aggravating their ulcers as they lay becalmed, or nearly so, outside a harbour with the tidal stream rushing out and the sun going down. Weather reports are not always reliable and one can never be sure of the wind, either its strength or direction. But the sailor usually can get some information whether to expect strong winds or light airs.

With tidal streams, you can be more confident. In tide tables or the local newspaper you can find the times of High Water and learn when the tidal stream will be flooding or ebbing and should not let yourself be caught outside a harbour, or a long way down the estuary when the ebb may halt your homecoming.

A brief discourse on tides will be appropriate just here. Primarily they are caused by the pull of the Moon and the Sun on the oceans. When both pull together, as at New Moon and Full Moon, we get what are known as Spring Tides, which means that for a period of two or three days, High Waters will be higher, and Low Waters lower than usual.

About a week later when the Moon comes to first or last quarters, the Moon and Sun are pulling in different ways and we get Neap Tides. We then experience High Waters which are not so high and Low Waters, not so low. There is less 'range' of tide.

Around the British Isles, High Water occurs twice a day, actually about every twelve and a half hours, and the time by the clock therefore is a little later each day. Low Water occurs about halfway between each High Water. (Having said this, it is quite in the cards that somebody will murmur 'Southampton'. I am trying to simplify the subject, remember? Southampton has DOUBLE TIDES but these are caused by geographical factors.)

When cruising, it is imperative that you should be constantly aware of the state of the tide. A sand or mud bank, for example, which you can cross at High Water, may be impassable at Low Water. If your boat is grounded while the tide is rising, you may get off again soon; if the tide is falling you may be stuck for several hours.

What will certainly affect you will be the flood stream or the ebb stream. As the tide rises from Low to High Water, the sea flows into harbours and estuaries; this is the flood stream and it is stronger at Springs than at Neaps. After High Water, the sea runs out again; this is the ebb stream. It is often boosted in strength by the current running down the river, especially after heavy rainfall.

Tidal streams are not just a matter of the sea running in and out of rivers and harbours. All round our coasts they present navigational problems.

Broadly speaking, the main flood streams follow two directions, one of which runs up the English Channel through the Straits of Dover and the other around the North of Scotland into the North Sea. The ebb streams, as you would expect, follow the reverse directions. When you 'poke your nose' out of many of our harbours, the flood or ebb stream racing along across the harbour entrance is encountered. Obviously, these tidal streams should be studied before you go out so that you may know what to expect. They are predicted for every time and place on charts and in tidal stream atlases.

On another, earlier page I discussed the techniques used when the boat is lying by a jetty. When you take up cruising, you will often find yourself riding to a mooring buoy or at anchor and at this time tidal streams may pose problems.

When a boat is lying at a buoy it is subjected to two influences; the wind and the water. When both are coming from the same direction, life is simple for the sailor. But this doesn't always happen. If the wind is light and the stream strong, the boat will probably lie to the stream. This is particularly so if the vessel is heavy and has a deep draught. Quite possibly, the wind may be blowing from aft; in which case your boat will be said to be 'tide-rode'. Then you will be faced with the problem of how to set your mainsail.

One method is to sail away under the foresail until you find enough clear water in which to round up and hoist the mainsail head to wind. Another is to emulate the example at the jetty and turn the boat round first, which can be done by reeving a slip-rope from aft through the ring of the buoy.

The problem recurs when you return to the buoy. It would be bad practice to try to pick up the buoy while going with the stream. The best method to adopt is to lower the mainsail while still head to wind and in a position abreast or to wind-

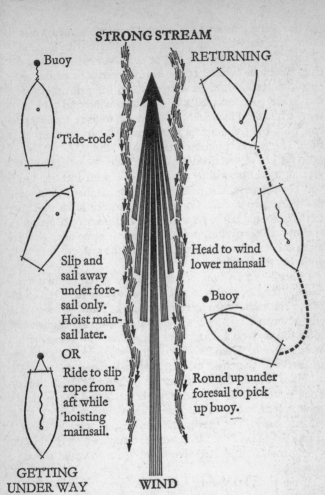

STRONG STREAM

RETURNING

Buoy

'Tide-rode'

Slip and
sail away
under fore-
sail only.
Hoist main-
sail later.

OR

Ride to slip
rope from
aft while
hoisting
mainsail.

GETTING
UNDER WAY

Head to wind
lower mainsail

Buoy

Round up under
foresail to pick
up buoy.

WIND

Fig 24. Tide and Stream

ward of the buoy; then to turn round under foresail only to
pick up the buoy head to stream.

I am dealing here with only straightforward cases, enough
to give you general principles. You will understand that there

can be endless permutations of these conditions, based on the strength of the wind and stream and on the relative directions of each. Of one thing you can be sure; you will never suffer from boredom because of too many repetitions of the same circumstances. You must keep in mind the principles; hoist and lower your mainsail while head to wind and pick up a buoy while head to stream. I advise you to use a small model and work out the different problems involved, in your spare time. This is good preparation for the real thing.

So far I have described the drill at a jetty or at a buoy. In a cruising boat you will be concerned also with anchors, but if you have grasped the principles I have defined, these need not worry you unduly. Coming to an anchor has a similarity to picking up a buoy. As a rule it is bad practice to let go an anchor when travelling with the stream; remember you are more concerned with your speed 'over the ground' than with your way through the water.

I once knew a young officer who was given his first command, a trawler, which he was ordered to take from the Humber to Harwich. When he arrived there he received a signal to anchor in such and such a position. He stopped engines and took the way off his ship but forgot he was going with a strong stream. When the anchor dropped there was a shower of sparks as the chain cable rattled and roared out over the windlass. There was consternation on the fo'c'sle and everybody scattered. But fortunately, the cable did not part; the trawler spun round to the stream like a top and after a while all was peace. The sparks and commotion were as nothing compared to his First Lieutenant's reaction which fixed in the young man's mind a resolve never again to make the same mistake.

If the wind is blowing against the stream as you enter harbour and approach anchorage, you may have to lower your mainsail while head to wind, then turn under foresail only to stem the stream before letting go the anchor.

A word or two about anchors is necessary. The best known type is the Admiralty pattern or fisherman's anchor pictured on crests, badges, picture postcards and almost anything with a nautical flavour. This type of anchor has been carried in ships and boats for centuries. It has two flukes, shaped rather like picks or spades, and when the anchor is on the bottom one of these digs into the mud; the other sticks above the bottom, which is a bad feature since this upper fluke may be fouled by the cable. In shallow water it also may damage the ship's bottom.

A long bar called a stock prevents the anchor from falling over sideways. When stowed onboard this stock can be dismantled and laid along the shank. When the stock is in place ready for anchoring, it is sometimes difficult to find a convenient stowage, so several new designs of anchor have come into general use. The stockless anchor became the universal fitting in modern ships because it can be hove up and stowed in a hawse-pipe and a small stockless anchor is nowadays in common use in small boats. Even when there is no hawse-pipe, it is still a relatively easy anchor to stow. When this anchor is on the bottom both flukes dig into the ground and the holding power is good.

Modern patent types which have appeared are the Danforth anchor which has some resemblance to the stockless anchor, and the C.Q.R. anchor which has a peculiar fitting not unlike a plough; this digs well into the bottom and gives excellent holding but it is rather awkward to stow on board.

Whatever type of anchor you use, it cannot do its job properly if it is not given the chance.

One requirement is that it should be given a horizontal pull while it is digging into the bottom. A nearly vertical pull will trip it out of the mud and it will drag. As a rule, once an anchor starts to drag, it will keep on doing so and there is nothing for it but to lay it again.

The horizontal pull is assisted by a proper cable. Chain throughout is always best but if you have a rope cable you can improve matters by inserting two or three fathoms of chain next to the anchor.

A further requirement, and it is essential, is that anchor and cable must be laid out correctly. The usual method in small boats is to cast the anchor while the boat is dropping slowly

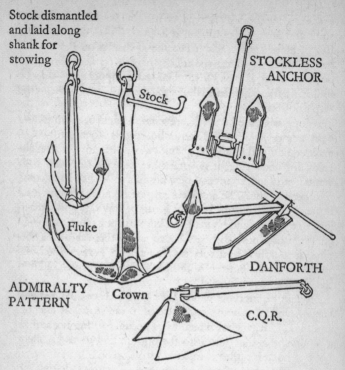

Stock dismantled and laid along shank for stowing

STOCKLESS ANCHOR

Stock

Fluke

ADMIRALTY PATTERN

Crown

DANFORTH

C.Q.R.

Fig 25. Types of Anchor

astern 'over the ground'; then to pay out the cable slowly so that there is no possibility of a bight of cable fouling the anchor.

A good tip, especially when the stream is strong, is to give the boat a good sheer over to one side when the anchor is dropped. The cable is then paid out across the flow of water. This gives a cushioning effect as you bring up and the bight of chain on the bottom improves the holding and prevents subsequent dragging.

The next requirement is to pay out enough cable in order to preserve the horizontal pull on the anchor. A good working rule is five times the depth of water. When all of this is chain cable you will have a good holding. It often used to be said by old sailors that 'the anchor held the cable and the cable held the ship'.

One more observation is necessary and this is that the holding power of the anchor and cable is influenced by the nature of the bottom. A hard, rocky bottom that does not allow the anchor to dig in is obviously bad; a mud bottom is generally good. So carefully pick the place where you are going to anchor. Spare a thought too for the depth of water and the state of the tide. Do not 'chuck' your anchor over in excessively deep water; the effect can be alarming. When in doubt, take a sounding. Also, do not anchor, if it can be avoided, in a place where you may find yourself aground at low water. Sometimes, when there is much rise and fall of tide, this can't be helped, and it may not be inconvenient if you are prepared for it. It is exasperating however, to come in to anchor and then just when you are changed to go ashore you find yourself surrounded by acres of mud.

These nice little problems, you will perceive, are part and parcel of the fascination of cruising under sail.

Chapter Twelve

Cruising
The Buoyage System

It is not often realised that the view from a small boat is very limited. Since the height of the eye is not much above sea-level, the circle of the horizon is only a short distance away. This is all related to the mathematics of the curvature of the Earth and I won't bother you with the formula but you can take it that if you work out the square root of your height of eye, in feet, the distance of your horizon is a little more than that answer, in miles. Say that your eye is five feet above the water, then the horizon will be less than three miles away, which is closer, I bet, than you guessed.

You will see objects beyond your horizon only if they themselves are high enough above sea-level. A floating baulk of timber three miles away would not be seen by the sailor, but the top of a lighthouse or tower forty feet high might be seen at nine or ten miles.

In an estuary or harbour that is bounded by cliffs or hills, you may have no difficulty in picking out objects, such as churches or chimneys, by which you can fix your position. But in flat country where the shores are low, you might quite easily get lost.

The lesson to be deduced from all this is that it is madness to take a small boat far from the shore, quite apart from ordinary considerations of weather and other risks. As you will not have much in the way of navigational equipment, fixing your position may become impossible and you will not know how to avoid shoals and other dangers.

It is beyond the scope of this book to present a course in pilotage and navigation, but I will give a few hints on the subject.

A good way to become acquainted with some of the principles is to get a chart of the locality in which you propose sailing. (I assume that you are taking the advice about not wandering far away from home until you know more about the hazards that might be encountered.)

Suppose this place is a small harbour and you are familiar with its lay-out. From the shore you have watched mud-banks appear as the tide falls and have seen them covered as the tide makes. Between the mudbanks you have seen channels meandering out to sea.

Now study the chart and compare this knowledge with what you see there. You will find the banks and shoals marked; you will see the channels between. You will note that the depths of water are marked in figures showing fathoms or feet. (The chart will tell you which are used in a phrase just under the title e.g. 'Soundings in fathoms'.) The depths as shown are related to a chart datum which is usually a very low water, so that the figures represent the least water you can expect at that position at any time.

There are also contour lines which link places of the same depth; these are similar to the contour lines describing hills and mountains in an atlas. On your chart they are, perhaps, the one-fathom line, the three-fathom line and others. There are, as well, symbols which tell you the nature of the bottom; M is for mud, R for rock, S for sand, and so on. There are several publications which give all the symbols employed.

As time goes by you will want to learn how to take bearings and plot them on a chart and will probably equip your boat with a small magnetic compass. Then you will have to learn

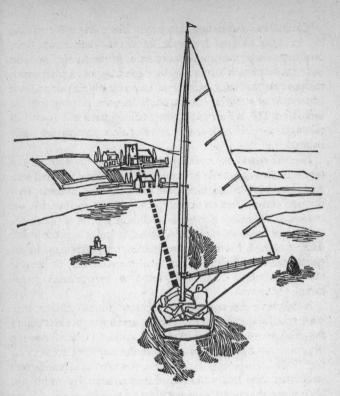

Fig 26. Leading Marks

things about deviation (caused by the magnetic influence of your boat) and variation (caused by the Earth's magnetic field.) All this, however, must come later. It is too much to begin with.

In the meantime you can learn to use your chart and make your way about the harbour by the use of transits and leading marks and buoys.

Applying your local knowledge to your chart you should learn to pick out buildings ahead or astern which are in line while you are proceeding along the deep channels. These we call 'transits'. A church steeple, say, in the distance, and the local gas-works, or other beauty spot, in the foreground. Or old Charlie's beach hut in line with the wing of Lord Hoozit's mansion on the hill. Notice that if you steer off to one side of the transit, the distant mark appears to move out towards the same side. This is the clue. These leading marks will guide you along the proper track at any state of tide whether the mud-banks are visible or not.

Leading marks are of the greatest value to the mariner and he uses them continually when entering or leaving harbour. And, besides keeping him clear of shoals and hazards, they can be a useful check on his compass.

As a further aid, buoys are commonly used to mark the limits and turns of the fairways and to warn of shoals and dangers. These buoys are invaluable to a yachtsman. In his small boat, some of the distant leading marks may be beyond his view, but if he can identify the buoys, he will know where he is.

Buoys have different shapes, superstructures, colours, top-marks, and sometimes bells, whistles and lights. At first glance they might seem to be just a bewildering array of floating ironmongery dropped into place at the whim of some crazy harbourmaster. Not so. Harbourmasters aren't built and don't work that way. Every buoy conforms to a system and if you understand the system your bewilderment will cease.

The system is related to the direction of the main stream of flood tide. In your local harbour, this means the direction of the stream when it is making into the harbour up to high water. If you were in the channel and entering the harbour (that is, going with the main stream of the flood tide) the edge of the channel on your right hand, that is your starboard hand, would be marked with starboard-hand buoys. The edge of the channel on your left hand, the port hand, would be marked with port-hand buoys. Needless to say, if you were leaving the harbour, you would be going against the direction of the main stream of flood-tide; so you would find starboard-hand buoys on your port hand and port-hand buoys on your star-

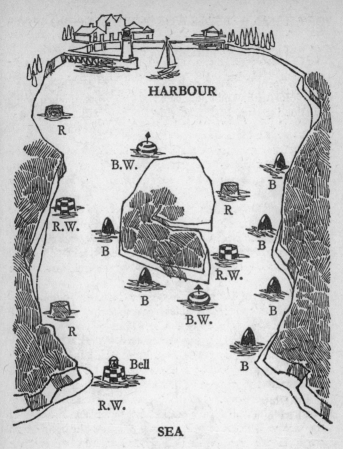

Fig 27. The Buoyage System

board-hand, which is not as ridiculous as it sounds, as a moment's reflection will show.

The important major classification therefore is: first, the starboard-hand buoy, which is a conical buoy having black in its colouring, and second, the port-hand buoy which is a can buoy whose predominant colour is red. Note carefully the

PORT HAND	MIDDLE GROUND	STARBOARD
(Can Buoys)	(Spherical)	(Conical)
Leave to Port when going with Main flood stream.	Mark ends of middle shoals. Pass either side.	Leave to Starboard when going with main flood stream.

Red

Black

Inner

Red and White
shows Red light

Outer

Black
White light

Red and White
chequered

Black and White
chequered

Fig 28. Buoys

shapes and the predominant colours and you will have an instant idea of where the channel lies in relation to the buoys; in other words, on which side to pass them. Sometimes the individual buoys have vertical white stripes or chequered painting and sometimes numbers and different top-marks to distinguish them one from another, but you must be sure which side of the channel they lie. A good mnemonic is the three syllables of the word 'conical' for 'starboard hand' and the two syllables 'can buoy' for 'port-hand'.

Occasionally there are shoals in the middle of a harbour and the fairways have to pass on both sides of them. The system still holds good. Whichever channel you use, you will come across the starboard-hand and port-hand buoys marking the limits of their channel as it passes these 'middle grounds'.

The spherical buoys marking the ends of these middle grounds usually have horizontal white stripes on their predominant colours; their top-marks are distinctive, diamond shapes at the inner ends of the shoals and triangular shapes at the seaward ends. Mariners used to remind themselves of these by saying 'We're going to sea for diamonds and coming home for Bass'. The symbols were the wrong way round, this being a piece of heavy sarcasm alluding to inadequate wages and the lack of beer at sea.

Chapter Thirteen
Thrills and Spills

Sailing is not the only sport one can think of which demands that enthusiasm shall be tempered with prudence. If you take up mountaineering, for instance, the golden rule must be to advance by sure and careful steps; patience and a conscientious study of the technique will get you to the top; hastiness and recklessness offer no future.

In the foregoing chapters I have suggested a series of careful steps by which the beginner may learn the technique of sailing a small boat. Firstly he was advised to become familiar with the general behaviour of all small boats; to get to understand how and why they float and how they should be handled. I suggested that this initial training can be safely undertaken on the local boating pond or any other stretch of quiet water.

Then I advanced by way of a little theory to the practical handling of a small sailing boat. The reader was initiated into the techniques of beating to windward, of tacking, of sailing on a reach and of running and gybing. Once again I urged caution and recommended plenty of practice on quiet and sheltered waters. Only after the new sailor had gained some experience and had developed some skill did I relax, like a fond parent, and let him become more venturesome.

This cautious approach was suggested because I believe it right to assert emphatically, from the start, that there are many hazards in boat sailing and indeed, in any form of boating. There are far too many accidents because of foolhardiness. Not long ago, for a sad example, I heard of a family that went out canoeing: there were several small children and their parents, not one of whom could swim. They did not wear lifejackets; and most of them were drowned. The disaster was blamed on swans, which were thought to have molested them!

Having said all this and put you, I hope into the right frame of mind, I will relax and reveal that many of the fears which may have attacked you hitherto are groundless. Indeed, the purpose of this book has been to show that sailing is not at all a mysterious and dangerous business, but rather a fascinating matter of craft, or if you like, 'know-how'. While I strongly disapprove of those who think it all too easy, that it is merely a matter of buying a boat, hoisting the sails and shoving off, I am anxious to encourage those who are eager and prepared to learn. I have seen many people, young and not so young, gazing wistfully at the passing sails. They want to take part but are afraid it is all too difficult. I wish to help such people.

I have concentrated so far on explaining the ways to keep a boat upright and afloat and this, after all, is my prime objective. Now I must break the news that you may not always be successful; it will, alas, surprise no one if, sometimes, you capsize. Don't let it surprise you too much; it isn't necessarily a disaster. Don't make a habit of it, of course, but there is no need to feel depressed and despondent if it does happen. I know some chaps who actually are inclined to boast of their capsizes; the truth being that they are keen dinghy racers who press their boats so hard to win races that often they take the odd chance too many.

If you capsize in a racing dinghy, or in many other types of light sailing boat, the drill is simple. One of the crew clambers over the high side of the boat and stands on the centre-plate.

This gives very effective leverage and brings the boat upright again. If it is done quickly enough, the crew can often resume the race after the extra water has been baled out.

Sailing, like all other human activities, has its moments of comedy. There was one member of our local yacht club, for example, who was quite nifty at this sort of thing. One day his boat took a spill and he was over the side in a flash. As it happened, though, the centre-plate hadn't been lowered so it wasn't there for him to stand on. The neat way in which he plummeted into the water and surfaced still provokes mirth when we talk about it in the bar.

Perhaps the first thing to bear in mind when your boat capsizes is that it is nearly always best to remain near the vessel. For one thing, most boats are equipped with buoyancy apparatus and will stay afloat for a long time; they offer good support. It is safer, believe me, to cling to the boat than to strike out for some distant shore.

A rescue craft will have less difficulty in locating a capsized boat than in finding a lone swimmer who has got far from it; even if it occurs to them to search.

Another good reason lies in the chance of righting your boat and getting it under way again. With light boats this is not as improbable as it may sound. Consider how you might tackle such a job.

The boat has gone over, for example, because you were caught by a sudden squall. The lee gunwale went under and in came the water. The chances are that the boat has gone over to an angle of about ninety degrees from the upright. The mast and spars have some buoyancy and tend to prevent her going further. The sails are wet and heavy and they will hamper any attempts to get the boat up again. Therefore, if you can reach the cleats or belaying pins, the first thing to do is to let go the main halyards. You may have to cut them, (which is one reason why you should always have a knife on you) but don't do this if is isn't necessary.

If you can work the sail down the mast or release it altogether, so much the better, but the important thing is to have the sail ready to come down quickly when the boat comes up.

You need not bother too much about the foresail because it isn't so heavy. Let it come down if you can, but don't cut the halyard; you may want to sail home with the foresail when you're upright again.

Now comes the business of getting the boat up. This is mostly a matter of using your weight to the best advantage. Standing on the centre-plate is a method I have already described. If another boat is handy, you may get a lift on the mast. But here is a point to watch. If you and all your crew exert your weight on the upper side with too much leverage, there is a chance that the boat will come upright and promptly fall over the other way. If you have two or three members in your crew, let one of them be handy to steady the boat from the low side.

The boat, you will be painfully aware, wants to flop all over the place because she is full of water and all stability has been lost. So your first and prompt care when the gunwales are clear is to get rid of that water as fast as you can.

At this moment you won't want to find you haven't a baler; either because you forgot to bring one or because it has fallen out. The lesson, of course, is that you should always have a baler with you and it should be secured with a lanyard, on board.

When the boat is upright, her buoyancy apparatus should prevent her being completely waterlogged and one of the crew ought to be able to get aboard. He should do this by climbing over the transom (the stern. See fig 1) not over the side. Once aboard he must work fast to shift that water.

In some boats an awkward snag arises when the top of the centre-plate case is still below the level of the water. The situation may remind you of those ghastly problems they give school-boys, where one pipe is filling a tank while another is letting the water out. You can't bale out while the water is free to come in through the centre-plate case. The only thing you can try is to plug the top of the case with rags or maybe your shirt until you have lowered the water level in the boat.

You are not, I need hardly say, now ideally set for a long voyage, but should be quite capable of sailing back home under the foresail, damp but determined. Provided you get enough water out of the boat to restore stability, you may even consider hoisting the mainsail again and letting it dry out.

The problem varies with different types of boat, and in the case of a heavy boat it may be impossible to do more than wait for assistance. The proximity of the shore or a river bank or even a patch of shaol water may, of course, offer a solution to your problems.

Enough has been said, I think, to show that a capsize is not the calamity which you might have supposed.

In conclusion, I wish to make it clear to my readers that he will never learn sailing merely by reading a book or even plenty of books. Progress in sailing will be decided by PRACTICE and perseverance in practice.

Some of the best helmsmen I know have been sailing for forty years; and they still don't know all the answers. Other first-class helmsmen have not been alive for half that number of years.

There is no need to let lack of years or a lack of experience stop any one from learning to sail a small boat.

Index

POCKET GUIDES

The key to leisure and learning.

Pocket Guides offer a new approach to a huge range of subjects and interests — from sailing to jazz.

They are concise, plentifully illustrated, inexpensive and informal — and each one is written by an expert in the subject.

The first six titles are:

Know Your Child's IQ   Glen Wilson and Diana Grylls
Wine Man's Bluff   Phoebe Hichens
Handywoman   Robert Tattersall
Chess for Beginners   R. G. Bellinger
Vegetables All the Year Round   C. E. F. Pryor
Sailing a Small Boat   Commander F. J. G. Hewitt, D.S.C.

And forthcoming titles include:

Jazz   Peter Clayton
Wine and No Nonsense   John Arlott
Making the Most of Your Money   Eamonn Fingleton
Tennis   P. C. J. Douglas
Yoga Exercises and Diet   Eve Diskin
Cycling   Frederick Alderson
Drawing   Jean H. Lunn
Riding   C. P. Agelasto
Woodwork   Antony Talbot
Astronomy   Iain Nicolson
Navigating a Small Boat   Commander F. J. G. Hewitt, D.S.C.

J. BARNICOAT
CASH SALES DEPT
P.O. BOX 11
FALMOUTH
CORNWALL TR10 9EN

Please send me the following titles

Quantity	SBN	Title	Amount
————			————
————			————
————			————
————			————
————			————
		TOTAL	————

Please enclose a cheque or postal order made out to **FUTURA PUBLICATIONS LIMITED** for the amount due, including 10p per book to allow for postage and packing. Orders will take about three weeks to reach you and we cannot accept responsibility for orders containing cash.

PLEASE PRINT CLEARLY

NAME..

ADDRESS...

....